Penguin Masterstudies

The White Devil *and* The Duchess of Malfi

Dr Sandra Clark was educated at Westfield College, University of London. As well as working in publishing she has taught at the University of Toronto and the Open University, and is currently a lecturer in English at Birkbeck College, University of London. She has published on Shakespeare and Elizabethan literature and her first book, *The Elizabethan Pamphleteers: Popular Moralistic Pamphlets 1580–1640*, came out in 1983. Sandra Clark is also the author of a critical study of *The Tempest* in the Penguin Masterstudies series.

Penguin Masterstudies
Advisory Editors: Stephen Coote and Bryan Loughrey

John Webster

The White Devil and *The Duchess of Malfi*

Sandra Clark

Penguin Books

Penguin Books Ltd, Harmondsworth, Middlesex, England
Viking Penguin Inc., 40 West 23rd Street, New York, New York 10010, U.S.A.
Penguin Books Australia Ltd, Ringwood, Victoria, Australia
Penguin Books Canada Ltd, 2801 John Street, Markham, Ontario, Canada L3R 1B4
Penguin Books (N.Z.) Ltd, 182–190 Wairau Road, Auckland 10, New Zealand

First published 1987

Made and printed in Great Britain by
Richard Clay Ltd, Bungay, Suffolk
Filmset in 9/11 pt Monophoto Times

Contents

General Introduction

1. John Webster

The life of the dramatist who wrote *The White Devil* and *The Duchess of Malfi*, plays which have won a reputation for tragedy second only to Shakespeare's, is much less well documented than most of those of his contemporary playwrights, and, despite recent discoveries, many facts about him remain obscure. It is not even absolutely certain when he was born, but it was probably about 1579 or 1580. He was the eldest son of John Webster, a London coach-builder, and Elizabeth Coates. Webster senior built up a prosperous business out of coach-making, which was then a relatively new and growing trade, catering for the rich and fashionable, as well as hiring out and building wagons and carts; the family lived, presumably rather comfortably, in West Smithfield, not far from Newgate prison, in the parish of St Sepulchre-without-Newgate, where John Webster senior was a leading citizen and one of the wealthiest men in the parish. This context has a certain relevance for the playwright whom T. S. Eliot has memorably described as 'much possessed by death', for the family business involved the hiring out of carts and wagons not only for theatrical purposes but also to transport condemned criminals from Newgate to execution on Tyburn Hill. Moreover, in 1605 Webster's father witnessed a document relating to the provision, through a will, for a great bell to be tolled at Newgate on the eve of executions, and for a hand-bell to be rung at midnight outside the cells of the condemned.

Given that his father had become a freeman of the Merchant Taylors' Company in 1571, Webster may well have attended the Merchant Taylors' School, where Kyd and Lodge had previously been pupils; it was a school with a strong Protestant tradition, as well as an established reputation in play-acting. He is probably that same 'Master John Webster, gentleman, son and heir apparent of John Webster of London, gentleman', who is recorded as entering the Middle Temple to study law in 1598. A spell at the Inns of Court, even if it did not result in a legal qualification (none is recorded for Webster), would explain the dramatist's knowledge of the law and interest in the theatrical aspects of courtroom scenes; it was not at all an unusual step for an educated young man to take. In fact two other young men who were to become playwrights and theatrical associates of Webster, John Marston and John Ford, studied at the Middle Temple at this time, and Webster may well have encountered them there.

His career, however, soon found its true direction, for in 1602, in an entry in the diary of Philip Henslowe, theatre-owner and financier, he is mentioned as collaborating with Munday, Drayton, Middleton and others on a play, now lost, called *Caesar's Fall.* Henslowe records four other payments to Webster for collaborative work in the same year. The next few years were spent in working with a range of dramatists, including Chettle, Heywood and Dekker, in addition to those already named. In 1603–4, he wrote an Induction, and perhaps some additional passages, for a new edition of Marston's popular Italianate tragicomedy, *The Malcontent,* a version written for performance by the King's Men, the best company of the day, with the great Richard Burbage in the title-role. His extant plays of the first decade of the seventeenth century consist of *Westward Ho!* and *Northward Ho!* (1604–5), a pair of city comedies, and *The Famous History of Sir Thomas Wyatt* (1607), a piece of Protestant propaganda, all written in collaboration with Dekker.

He shows no inclination towards tragedy, and *The White Devil,* written sometime between 1609 and 1612, comes as a surprise in this opus. Webster was disappointed by its reception, as the preface to the reader in the printed edition shows. 'It was acted,' he wrote, 'in so dull a time of winter, presented in so open and black a theatre, that it wanted (that which is the only grace and setting out of a tragedy) a full and understanding auditory.' The theatre was probably the Red Bull in Clerkenwell, a public playhouse with a somewhat rowdy reputation where the audience was accustomed to less sophisticated entertainment. Webster did, however, take the unprecedented step of praising the 'well approved industry' of one of the actors, Richard Perkins, who probably played Flamineo and was later to become a leading figure in his troupe, the Queen's Men.

With his next play, *The Duchess of Malfi,* written soon afterwards, he took the precaution of offering it to the rival company, the King's Men, which represented a theatrical advance; they had recently and successfully staged a number of plays requiring spectacular effects, such as *Macbeth, The Tempest, Henry VIII, The Two Noble Kinsmen,* and *The Second Maiden's Tragedy.* The play was first put on, probably in the winter of 1613–14, at the indoor theatre used by the King's Men, the Blackfriars, and subsequently at the Globe. Burbage played Ferdinand, and John Lowin, another leading actor of the day, Bosola. Whoever played the Duchess, whether Richard Sharp, then only eleven or twelve, whose name is assigned to the role in the first printed edition of the play of 1623, or Richard Robinson, the main boy-actor of the company, he scored a particular success, for the pathos and conviction of the performance are mentioned in commendatory verses by Middleton and Rowley prefixed to the text. Middleton, admiring what he calls 'this masterpiece of tragedy', wrote:

> Thy epitaph only the title be,
> Write, *Duchess*, that will fetch a tear for thee,
> For who e'er saw this *Duchess* live, and die,
> That could get off under a bleeding eye?

The play seems right away to have been regarded as Webster's masterpiece, and it has enjoyed continuous stage success, sometimes in adapted versions, from the Restoration to the present day.

Between his two great tragedies Webster wrote a poem, 'A Monumental Column', to commemorate the death of Prince Henry in 1612. He dedicated it to Robert Carr, Viscount Rochester, the King's current favourite, perhaps in an effort to secure well-placed patronage. It has many similarities of thought and phrasing to *The Duchess of Malfi* and Webster was probably working on them both at the same time. After *The Duchess of Malfi* he wrote a comedy, now lost, called *The Guise*, of which he thought very highly, a group of prose 'characters' for the sixth edition of the work known as Sir Thomas Overbury's *Characters*, printed in 1615 after Overbury's death, one more play as a solo effort, *The Devil's Law-Case* (? 1617), and a number of collaborative works including *Appius and Virginia* (? 1624, though possibly much earlier), *Keep the Widow Waking* (1624) and *A Cure for a Cuckold* (c. 1625). His latest published work was a civic pageant, *Monuments of Honour* (1624).

Very little is known of Webster's life outside the theatre. He married Sara Peniall in 1606, when she was six months pregnant, and they had at least five children. His father died in 1615, and it is likely that he would have come in for a legacy, for by this time the business, built up with the help of Webster's younger brother Edward, was flourishing impressively. His known dramatic output is certainly not large enough to suggest that this was his sole means of support. M. C. Bradbrook, in *John Webster Citizen and Dramatist*, conjectures that his interests changed after this time, particularly in the direction of a greater involvement with the world of commerce. He became a freeman of the Merchant Taylors' company like his father, which testifies to a certain standing in the life of the city, and his later writing shows an increased use of legal satire. There are few contemporary references to Webster in his lifetime. Henry

Fitzgeffrey provides the only picture of the dramatist in an unflattering description in his satirical poem, 'Notes from Blackfriars', printed in *Certain Elegies by Sundry Excellent Wits* (1617), calling him 'crabbed Websterio,/The playwright-cartwright (whether either)', an allusion puzzling to commentators until the recent discovery of the Webster family business in coach and cart-building. Orazio Busino, an Italian envoy to London, recorded in 1618 a rather confused account of scenes from *The Duchess of Malfi*, which he objected to for religious reasons. It may be assumed that the play was performed in that year. Apart from the commendatory verses to *The Duchess of Malfi* printed in 1623, this is about all that survives. Even the date of Webster's death is not known. He is referred to in the past tense in Thomas Heywood's poem *The Hierarchy of the Blessed Angels* in 1634, from which it is conjectured that he was by then dead.

2. Contexts Social and Historical

The Italian courts of Webster's two tragedies, though based on historical or semi-historical accounts of actual courts in sixteenth-century Italy, and at the same time seriously influenced by that potent Elizabethan Italy-of-the-mind, the setting for so many tragedies of blood, have also a significant relationship with the English court at the time the plays were written. A strong anti-courtly tradition in literature had become established in the days of Elizabeth, when even a poet like Spenser could represent court life not only as the seed-bed of courtesy and virtue but also as a rat-race where each person vied with the next to gain a place on the golden ladder of preferment held out by a vicious and unprincipled Princess (in *The Faerie Queene*, II.vii). The poetic satires of Donne and Marston, written at the turn of the century, ushered in an age of scepticism as to the validity of the myth of the court as a centre of moral value and the courtier as the embodiment of civilized virtue; this scepticism was to intensify when James I came to the throne. Court corruption had already been presented as a dramatic theme in the work of Marston in *Antonio's Revenge* (*c*. 1600) but it gained in topicality and specificity with the arrival of the new King. The discrepancy between the monarch's known interest in the philosophy of government and the actuality of life at his court provided dramatists with a rich source of irony for their representations of corruption in the courts of Princes. For James kept a court where the power of flatterers and favourites was notorious, gross and vulgar behaviour common, and the King's irresponsible dispensation of honours and titles legendary. Marston caught something of its flavour in *The Malcontent,* a tragi-comedy for which Webster wrote the Induction; this is a dark and bitter vision of the misuse of power, despite its conclusion in a restoration of order. *The Fawn* (? 1604), perhaps Marston's next play, is more genial in temper, but it depicts a court rife with scandal, gossip and sexual malpractice, ruled by a Duke who is a self-deceived, self-admiring fool.

Not only was the reputation of James I's court – widely commented on in letters and contemporary gossip – a low and scandalous one generally, but there were specific examples of misdemeanour and malpractice in court circles which seem to have influenced the moral climate of much contemporary drama, not least Webster's. The story of Sir Thomas Overbury is a case in point. Overbury, a powerful figure at court and secretary to the King's dissolute favourite, Robert Carr – it was said that Carr ruled the King, and Overbury ruled Carr – was poisoned in 1613 at the instigation of Carr's new wife, Lady Frances Howard, because he opposed the marriage. Webster may well have known Overbury personally, perhaps meeting him at the Middle Temple; he dedicated his poem, 'A Monumental Column', to Carr, and contributed a substantial number of new 'characters' to the sixth edition of Overbury's *Characters* (1615), which he may even have edited. Frances Howard, one of several notorious women of high birth and equivocal reputation in James's reign, was first married, probably in part by royal arrangement, to the young Earl of Essex in 1606, amid great splendour at court, with a spectacular masque, *Hymenaei,* provided by Ben Jonson and Inigo Jones to celebrate the occasion. Five years later the ambitious Frances with the support of her family sought to divorce Essex, giving as her grounds non-consummation of the marriage, in order to become the wife of Robert Carr, whose star was then very much in the ascendant. The King had to set up a special panel of bishops to testify to Frances's virginity; divorce and re-marriage were accomplished, but not without opposition. Overbury, hitherto Carr's supporter, spoke out against the marriage and in 1613 was thrown into the Tower. Over a long period of more than a year he was gradually poisoned by means of food doctored by Frances and her assistants and conveyed to him in prison; he died in 1614. In 1616 Frances and Robert Carr, Earl and Countess of Somerset, were put on trial in Westminster Hall for Overbury's murder. They were found guilty, but reprieved, and it was, predictably, the underlings and accessories who went to the gallows. Mistress Turner, who had acted as Frances's accomplice throughout, is recorded as declaiming against the court from the scaffold:

O the court, the court! God bless the king and send him better servants about him, for there is no religion in most of them but malice, pride, whoredom, swearing and rejoicing in the fall of others. It is so wicked a place as I wonder the earth did not open and swallow it up. Mr Sheriff, put none of your children thither.

The Overbury affair was outstandingly scandalous, but its sordid quality and the involvement of the monarch in affairs of the deepest moral squalor were not unique.

If Frances Howard embodied a real-life 'white devil', whose career was no less extraordinary than Vittoria's (although the full extent of her criminality was of course not known to Webster until after he had written his tragedies), then it is also possible to find contemporary examples of great ladies whose marriages, in various ways, were as shocking and sometimes as unfortunate as the Duchess of Malfi's. Frances Brandon, Countess of Suffolk, married her secretary and groom of the chamber, who was sixteen years her junior, and caused adverse comment from the Queen. Ann More, daughter of Sir Thomas Egerton, the Lord Keeper of England, married the aspiring poet John Donne, was thrown (briefly) into prison, and endured years of poverty for the sake of her love-match. Penelope Devereux, Sidney's Stella and another member of the Essex family, was married in 1581 to Lord Rich, a man whom she did not love; she endured more than twenty years with him until 1605, when they were divorced, and she was secretly re-married to her longstanding lover, Charles Blount, amid scandal, because it was against the canons of the Church and the wishes of the King. These histories form a background to Webster's play, but there are others which stand in a closer relationship. These are several episodes in contemporary history in which the central situation of *The Duchess of Malfi* seems to be significantly outlined. It would be dangerous to make too much of these, by implying either that they directly influenced Webster's choice and treatment of his subject, or else that he deliberately intended allusions to them through his play. But they are stories which Webster is very likely to have known, and their resemblances to the history of the Duchess and Antonio lend it a greater poignancy.

Very close to home was the plight of Lady Arbella Stuart, a Scottish noblewoman and cousin to the King, after the royal children next in line of succession to the throne. Despite the fact that a succession of marriages had been proposed for this dangerously well-born lady ever since she was eight, with James himself at one time a possibility, she remained unmarried until 1610 when, at the age of thirty-five, she contracted a secret union with William Seymour, who was eleven years younger. Only the previous year James had expressly forbidden a union between the couple, not because William was, like Antonio in the play, of low rank, but rather the contrary; as a member of the great Seymour family, grandson to Edward, Earl of Hertford, his high birth did in fact strengthen the claim to the throne of Arbella and any children of their union. The clandestine marriage was discovered in a matter of weeks and the couple imprisoned in the Tower. They managed to escape, Arbella in male disguise, in 1611, but she was recaptured halfway across the channel to France, though William got away. She was brought back to the Tower, where she languished, ill and half mad, till her death in 1615. These events were known to the general public, and the King was regarded as callous in his treatment of his cousin, whose unhappy fate became for a time a subject for popular ballad-mongers. The resemblances of this story to Webster's play need not be exaggerated but they certainly exist, and the fact that the events were taking place at the very time of *The Duchess of Malfi*'s composition may well support a theory of influence. A story of a slightly different kind is that of the poet Torquato Tasso, who is actually quoted by name in the play. Tasso had been shut up in a madhouse by Alfonso D'Este, Duke of Ferrara, in 1579, because he was in fact insane. But a legend had grown up, known in England by Webster's time, that he had been imprisoned because of a love-affair with a Princess of high rank, as the poet Ovid was supposed to have been banished by the Emperor Augustus for the same reason (a subject recently given comic treatment by Ben Jonson in *The Poetaster*); this Princess came to be identified with Leonora D'Este, Alfonso's sister. Several elements in this tale, the setting in an Italian court, the misalliance of a Duke's sister, the imprisonment among madmen as the lover's punishment, all recall Webster's play, and again the resemblances are poignant ones.

Finally, the story of Antonio Perez, a brilliant Spaniard involved in espionage on a European scale, both working for Philip II of Spain and also intriguing with the Flemish and the Portuguese, sheds an interesting light on Webster's depiction of court intrigue as well as perhaps bearing a more specific relation to *The Duchess of Malfi*. Perez was eventually imprisoned and sentenced to death by Philip, who stood in some danger from information and documents that Perez possessed which incriminated him in various subversive activities, including assassination; but he escaped and went into exile in France at the court of Henry IV, who used him on a mission to England. Less fortunate was the widowed Princess of Eboli, his ally, rumoured to be his lover, and former wife to his first protector, one of the greatest ladies of Spain; Philip threw her into prison in 1579, at the same time that Perez was captured, where she suffered increasingly severe confinement without ever being charged with a specific crime. Like the Duchess of Malfi she maintained her dignity throughout a long period of suffering and humiliation, keeping with her her faithful attendants and her youngest child. She was never released, but lived on for nearly thirteen years, confined solely by the will of a tyrannical King to a single barred and darkened room, where she died in 1592. Perez visited England in 1593 and stayed for two years, under the patronage of the Earl of Essex; he took part in public life and in espionage activities on Essex's behalf. He became a public figure of some notoriety, and his story and connection with the Princess of Eboli were known through his own published account, *Pedacos de historia o Relaciones* (1594), and other works; but his position, as a Spanish double-agent, was always insecure, and when James, who wished to cultivate an alliance with Spain, came to the throne, Perez was banished from the country. He died in 1611.

These stories of scandal, crime, suffering and torture amongst Princes were recent history, in some cases contemporary events to Webster and the Jacobean dramatists; it can be seen from them that the sort of events depicted in tragic drama of the period were not utterly remote from what had been known to happen in Renaissance courts. Needless to say, however, Webster's tragedies owe as much to literary and theatrical tradition as to life, and must be seen in terms of their theatrical as well as their social context. During the earlier years of his career as a playwright, despite recurrent outbreaks of plague which closed the playhouses for months at a time between 1603 and 1610, the London theatre scene was exceptionally lively and dynamic. Webster evolved some of the themes which were to dominate his two tragedies – the connections between marriage and money, the place of women within the context of a social and a family hierarchy, the relationship of the world of the play to real life – in the writing of his city comedies in collaboration with other playwrights. But he was attentive to the work of his contemporaries, and readily absorbed theatrical ideas, devices, techniques and even phrases from a variety of sources. In the preface to the reader printed with *The White Devil* in 1612 Webster praises the work of several named contemporaries, implying their influence on his own; he mentions

that full and height'ned style of Master Chapman, the labour'd and understanding works of Master Jonson: the no less worthy composures of the both worthily excellent Master Beaumont, and Master Fletcher: and . . . the right happy and copious industry of Master Shakespeare, Master Dekker, and Master Heywood.

There is one significant omission from this list, the name of Marston, perhaps because this playwright had retired from the theatre and taken holy orders before *The White Devil* was written; but Marston's work, along with Shakespeare's, is probably the most deeply influential on Webster's. Webster probably knew Marston personally, another Inns of Court contact, and the more experienced playwright may have been doing him a favour in asking him to write an Induction, after the manner of Jonson in *Every Man Out of his Humour* (1598), for a new edition of *The Malcontent* in 1604. This play, along with *Antonio's Revenge*, was a seminal influence on tragic and tragi-comic writing for the next decade. Webster especially drew on Marston's depiction of Italianate court corruption, his alienated malcontent figures and his brilliantly inventive theatricality, with its exploitation of music, masque, dumbshows and other spectacular effects, its ghosts, madness and grotesque violence. The tone and atmosphere of Marston's plays, his handling of imagery, particularly of animals and disease or poison, his sensationalism and his bold deployment of 'horrid laughter', are all reflected in Webster's tragedies.

The relationship of Shakespeare to Webster may be seen in two ways, both general and specific. It has been said that Webster is the only dramatist, apart from Shakespeare, who consistently develops patterns of iterative imagery so as to extend the meanings of the action. H. T. Price, in his article, 'The Function of Imagery in Webster', says that Webster 'makes consistent use of a double construction, an outer and an inner. He gives us figure in action and figure in language. These he fuses so intimately as to make the play one entire figure.' That this is a direct result of Shakespeare's influence seems unlikely, since it is so integral to Webster's dramatic method that the resemblance must come from similar habits of mind and attitudes towards dramatic language rather than a technique consciously acquired. Perhaps the same could be said about Webster's tragedies as tragedies of character. With the exception of Middleton, whose two great tragedies, *The Changeling* and *Women Beware Women*, post-date Webster, there is no other dramatist in whom the tragic effect is so dependent on character. This is less true of *The White Devil* than of *The Duchess of Malfi* but even so Vittoria, Brachiano and Flamineo are endowed, along with the Duchess, Bosola and Ferdinand, with a kind of personality and selfhood that makes them unlike, say, the characters of Marston's plays or *The Revenger's Tragedy* or Beaumont and Fletcher's tragedies; and it is the expression of this self-hood that not only brings about their fates but also involves the audience emotionally in their suffering. There are few tragic characters of the

15

period fit to be compared with, say Othello or Macbeth, but Webster's protagonists can stand the comparison.

Examples of specific Shakespearian influence are easier to pinpoint. *The White Devil* clearly owes much to *Hamlet*; Cornelia's madness imitates Ophelia's (with some darker touches from Lady Macbeth and King Lear). Francisco's revenger's soliloquy, during which Isabella's ghost appears to him (IV.i.77–125), draws together phrases and motifs from several of Hamlet's, while Flamineo's madness and malcontent nature, the two ghosts and the feeling of approaching doom recall both *Hamlet* and the genre of revenge tragedies related to it. *Antony and Cleopatra*, though not yet in print, may have been a source of inspiration for Brachiano and Vittoria's love-affair, particularly Brachiano's initial absorption in his passion and the sudden changes of mood in IV.ii. Possibly *Othello*, another yet-unpublished play, was in Webster's mind when he had Francisco disguise himself as a Moorish soldier 'experienc'd in state affairs or rudiments of war'; more certainly the death of the Duchess of Malfi, with her brief and poignant revival to utter two words to Bosola, echoes that of innocent Desdemona, as Bosola's self-lacerating anguish over her body recalls Othello's remorse. It may have been under the influence of Shakespeare's structural experiment in *Antony and Cleopatra*, whereby one of the two main characters dies at the end of the fourth act and leaves the other to sustain the interest of the last act alone, that Webster designed the early death of his Duchess. There are recollections of *Macbeth*, in the tension and atmosphere of Antonio's nocturnal confrontation with Bosola in II.iii. and, as in almost all tragedy in the revenge tradition, of *Hamlet*, in Bosola's meditations on human insignificance, and the Cardinal's belated sense of guilt. Several moments from *Hamlet* converge in the scene of Antonio's ill-fated last entry to the Cardinal's chamber in Act V; it is Antonio who is given lines that echo Hamlet in his desire to kill Claudius when he is not in a state of grace (though Antonio's intention seems to be the opposite of Hamlet's):

> Could I take him
> At his prayers there were hope of pardon
>
> (V.iv.42–3)

but it is Bosola who comes up from behind to deal the death-blow:

> Fall right my sword:
> I'll not give thee so much leisure as to pray.
>
> (V.iv.44–5)

Webster's plays belong to the mode of revenge tragedy (as will be discussed later) and show clear influence of three of the greatest plays in this style, Marston's *Antonio's Revenge*, *Hamlet* and *The Revenger's Tragedy*. They have been seen (by J. W. Lever, in *The Tragedy of State*, 1971) as a deliberate return to the Italianate settings of Marston after the different styles of tragedy explored by Jonson in his classical plays, *Sejanus* and *Catiline*, and Chapman in his tragedies based on French Renaissance history. *The White Devil* and *The Duchess of Malfi* follow on from a long series of tragedies of blood initiated by Kyd's epoch-making *The Spanish Tragedy* (? 1587), and by their time some of the conventions of revenge tragedy had become old-fashioned or over-familiar, so that, if he used them at all, Webster either modified them considerably or else implied a self-consciousness in the way he handled them. For instance, in *The White Devil*, Francisco's soliloquy in IV.i., where he decides to take on the role of revenger of his sister's murder, seems deliberately to mock and play with the whole concept of tragedy of revenge, to the extent of almost undermining the seriousness of the play. When Francisco says, 'Come, to this weighty business' (IV.i.118), it is almost as if the actor might wink at the audience or humorously sigh at the idea of being in a play where the procedure is so familiar. 'My tragedy must have some idle mirth in't/Else it will never pass', he continues; the playwright points out to the audience that he knows they are as accustomed as he to the sort of techniques and situations that are *de rigueur* in a play like this. In *The Duchess of Malfi* Bosola says that Antonio met his death by 'such a mistake as I have often seen/In a play' (V.v.95–6). By allowing his character this kind of self-consciousness Webster is taking considerable risks; yet although there are moments when the audience is almost invited to sit back objectively in the conscious-ness that this is 'only a play' and even the characters know it, this impulse towards critical detachment is balanced against a stronger one towards involvement. For all his scepticism, Webster does reanimate the conventions of revenge tragedy so that one is stimulated by his use of them and absorbed into the fictional worlds of his plays.

The revenge mode was in fact far from dead, though the tragedies following Webster which drew upon it, by Middleton and Ford for example, show very different attitudes towards evil, and towards the relation of crime and society with which a play like Kyd's *The Spanish Tragedy* was concerned. The plays no longer focus on a revenger whose task it is to set right a whole society 'out of joint' (*Hamlet*); now the revenger often tends to act against, rather than on behalf of, the interests of order and social justice, but the victims of the revenger are not necessarily more sympathetic. The distribution of guilt and innocence is not clear-cut. Webster 'repudiates the simple values of the Revenge play' (J. R. Mulryne, *'The White Devil* and *The Duchess of Malfi'* in *Jacobean Theatre*, Stratford-upon-Avon Studies, I, 1960), in the sense of an appeal to pity and instinctive justice at the outrage of the murders committed, and aims instead for a representation of the complexity, and even sometimes the unfathomable nature of human motivation. U. Ellis-Fermor sees Webster as a transitional figure between early and late Jacobean drama in that his work combines an intimate preoccupation with death with moments of spiritual illumination:

He remains the playwright who most clearly perceived the chaos and conflict in which the tragic thought of his generation was caught and, while unable to climb out of the 'deep pit of darkness', discerned for a moment through the eyes of one of his characters the 'stars' that 'shine still'.

(The Jacobean Drama, p. 170, 1936, 1965)

He wrote the 'last Jacobean tragedies of heroic proportion' (R. Ornstein, *The Moral Vision of Jacobean Tragedy,* 1960), even taking the daring step of using weak and wilful women as his embodiments of heroism. The tragedies of Middleton and Ford are as much concerned as Webster's with moral anarchy and evil in society, but they are without the supreme moments of defiance and self-expression which, however painful and agonized, give Webster's plays a lasting grandeur.

The White Devil

1. Title

The title of the play was proverbial, but its meaning is not a single or specific one. The proverb, 'The white devil is worse than the black,' is recorded as current from the late 1590s, and it meant that a devil in disguise, that is, one not in its natural colour of black, was a more potent force for evil than a devil who was instantly recognizable. The conception has been thought to originate from two passages in the Bible:

Wo be to you, Scribes and Pharises, hypocrites: for ye are like unto whited tombes, which appeare beautifull outward, but are within full of dead mens bones, and all filthines.

(St Matthew XXIII:27. The Geneva Bible, 1581)

For such are false apostles, deceitful workers, transforming themselves into the apostles of Christ.
And no marvel; for Satan himself is transformed into an angel of light.

(II Corinthians XI:13, 14)

Luther, a powerful influence on sixteenth-century Protestant writers, distinguished between white and black devils in his Latin *Commentary on The Epistle of St Paul to the Galatians* (1535), referring to the white devil as the source of spiritual sin, which may appear like goodness but is far more damnable than fleshly sin:

In spirituall matters, where Sathan commeth forth, not blacke but white in the likenes of an Angell or of God himselfe, there he passeth himselfe with most craftie dissimulation and wonderfull sleights, and is wont to set forth to sale his most deadly poison for the doctrine of grace.

(*A Commentary of M. Doctor Martin Luther Upon the Epistle of S. Paul to the Galatians*, London, 1535, f. 21r.)

There are many early-seventeenth-century examples of the expression meaning a hypocrite, or apparently respectable person who turns out to have hidden vices. A sermon preached by Thomas Adams at Paul's Cross in 1613 was entitled 'The White divell, or the Hypocrite uncased', and in a version of this sermon published in 1615 Adams identified the white devil not with Satan but with Judas, betrayer of Christ. The sermon seems to have been influenced if not inspired by Webster, and contains verbal echoes of both *The White Devil* and *The Duchess of Malfi*. In the play, the title most obviously refers to Vittoria. She is several times called a devil, and in IV.ii, when Brachiano believes her to have betrayed him, he exclaims against her:

> Your beauty! O, ten thousand curses on't.
> How long have I beheld the devil in crystal?
>
> (IV.ii.87–8)

The interpretation of the white devil as an apparent angel of light who brings men to destruction is clearly appropriate to her, but the other notion of the white devil as Judas or betrayer relates better to another character, Cardinal Monticelso. Monticelso's public role of religious adviser and spokesman for accepted morality, when he lectures Brachiano in II.i on his duties as Prince and father, censures Vittoria as a whore and rebukes Lodovico in IV.iii for contemplating revenge, contrasts with his more vicious and venial private self, which is, at least until IV.iii, the strongest force in the play for revenge against Vittoria and Brachiano. He is also an advocate of concealed action. He advises Francisco:

> We see that undermining more prevails
> Than doth the cannon. Bear your wrongs conceal'd,
> ... till the time be ripe
> For th'bloody audit, and the fatal gripe.
>
> (IV.i.13–19)

Monticelso, Cardinal and subsequently Pope, head of the Church, wields his immense power like the Antichrist, a devil in robes of religious authority. The fact that the play's title can refer, in different ways, to two opposed characters who are bitter enemies throughout is one of many factors which complicate but also enrich our response to the play.

2. Sources

The plot of the play is based on historical fact and events that were relatively recent at the time of writing. The life of Paolo Giordano Orsini, lord of Brachiano, and his affair with Vittoria Accoramboni were extremely well documented, and modern research has uncovered an immense quantity of manuscript material relating to them. Almost all of this was unknown to Webster, however, and despite scrupulous efforts by modern scholars it has not been possible to discover a primary source for the play. There is a contemporary manuscript account of the affair of Brachiano and Vittoria and their murders which resembles Webster's play in the ways that it differs from historical fact and from other contemporary accounts; it is a newsletter written by an Italian agent to the German banking house of Fugger, known as the Fugger newsletter, and extant only in German. In all probability this German manuscript derives from an Italian original and, according to the theories of Gunnar Boklund, the expert on Webster's sources, it is this lost Italian version which Webster used. He also knew a pamphlet in English, *A Letter Lately Written from Rome*, which came out in 1585, the year of Brachiano's and Vittoria's deaths. It was translated from Italian and probably written or compiled by John Florio, whose translation of Montaigne's *Essays* was also an important source for Webster, and it provided Webster with details for his presentation of the conclave scene, for the new Pope's unhistorical refusal to encourage revenge on Vittoria and Brachiano, and for his pronouncement of excommunication. He may well also have used a contemporary Italian history, such as that by C. Campana, *Delle historie del mondo* (1596), which describes the manner of Vittoria's death, and gives details of Lodovico's career. In 1600–1601 Brachiano and Isabella's surviving son, Virginio Orsini, who appears in the play as Giovanni, was entertained at Elizabeth's court over the Christmas period, an event which might well have aroused Webster's interest. Although the historical facts concerning the lives of Brachiano, Vittoria and the other characters in the story are considerably different from the circumstances in Webster's play, it is not correct to assume that he deliberately changed all of them to suit his dramatic purposes. He undoubtedly knew fewer details about the real lives of these people than modern scholars do. The story that he knew, though it differs in many respects from the true one, is much as follows.

Paolo Giordano Orsini, born probably in 1537, married Isabella, daughter of Cosimo de Medici, in 1558. Their union brought together two of Italy's most powerful families, and produced a son, Giovanni. Paolo Giordano subsequently fell in love with Vittoria Accoramboni, a beautiful gentlewoman who was married to a nephew of Cardinal Montalto. She refused his advances until they were free to marry, so that he accordingly had his wife and her husband murdered. Vittoria's husband was murdered by her brother Marcello. After this deed, Vittoria and Paolo Giordano lived together, but their union was opposed by both Medicis and Orsinis as a misalliance between a great Duke and a woman of lower status. They did, however, marry after an enforced separation, but when Cardinal Montalto became Pope, under the name of Sixtus V, he banished Paolo Giordano from Rome forever. The couple

21

retired to Padua and held court there, but shortly afterwards Paolo Giordano died, probably in suspicious circumstances, in 1585. Vittoria very soon found herself at odds with his powerful family over the settlement of the will and they had her murdered while at prayers in her house at Padua, together with her brother Flamineo. The deed was carried out by Lodovico Orsini, a relative of Paolo Giordano and also a soldier and notorious murderer, who was subsequently strangled in prison. This largely unhistorical story is a little reminiscent in its violence and brutality of the crude tale of love and murder which Shakespeare found in Cinthio's *Hecatommithi*, and used as the basis for *Othello*. They are essentially the same kind of story, and although Webster's plot may have derived an extra soupçon of excitement from the fact that one of the real-life participants had visited the capital recently, it is not likely that a Jacobean audience would have distinguished between the two plays on the grounds of historical truth.

However, the facts which Webster did not know are no less randomly violent. The real-life Paolo Giordano probably had his wife Isabella strangled several years before he ever met Vittoria. Isabella had led a notoriously scandalous private life, and it was thought by some that her children were not fathered by her husband. Paolo Giordano and Vittoria were married in a secret and irregular ceremony very soon after he had arranged the murder of her husband, Francesco Peretti, a young man, with help of one of her many brothers, a bandit known as Mancino. The couple were forbidden to live together by the Pope, Gregory XIII, and spent a considerable portion of the few years of their union apart, although they had a second secret wedding two years after the first, and a third and public ceremony the next year. Three ceremonies were deemed necessary to secure Vittoria's right to the title of Duchess of Brachiano. On the very day of this third ceremony Cardinal Montalto's election to the Papacy was announced. The couple at once left Rome, escaping from the Pope's jurisdiction to live in the republic of Venice, but later in the year Paolo Giordano died, of natural causes, at Salo on Lake Garda. He had been hugely corpulent, and a sufferer from gout. Vittoria, insisting on her rights to a substantial part of her husband's property, was murdered a few months later by a gang of banditti in the pay of Lodovico Orsini, who was not present at her death.

Webster had much to do to transform the story of Brachiano and Vittoria into a revenge tragedy. As with *The Duchess of Malfi*, he took material from a number of sources, sometimes quoting almost verbatim from his originals in a way that has caused scholars to censure him disapprovingly for laziness. Perhaps he looked specifically for Italianate colouring, because in certain examples of this he took details for a single scene or incident from works he did not use elsewhere. For instance, from Erasmus's dialogue *Funus* from *Colloquia Familiaria* he took a passage, almost word for word, for the Latin dialogue between Lodovico and Gasparo in V.iii when they torment the dying Brachiano in their disguise as Capuchin monks. For the account of the Papal election in IV.iii he drew on an English translation of a French work, Hierome Bignon's *A Briefe, but an Effectual Treatise of the Election of Popes* (1605), which supplied details of procedure that Webster preferred to those given in *A Letter Lately Written from Rome*. The ingenious manner of Brachiano's murder by a poisoned helmet he probably took from an English translation of Pierre Boaistuau's *Theatrum Mundi* (translated in 1581), a collection of moralized stories used by other dramatists of the period, including Shakespeare. The drama of his contemporaries was also a source of inspiration. Cornelia's madness in V.iv is clearly based on Ophelia's in *Hamlet*, down to the herbs, rosemary and rue, which she hands out to Flamineo, and the same play also provided phrases and motifs for Francisco's revenger's soliloquy in IV.i, Flamineo's antic disposition, the two ghosts and the death-laden atmosphere of *The White Devil*'s last act. Verbal echoes of *King Lear*, *Macbeth* and perhaps *Troilus and Cressida* can also be found. *Antony and Cleopatra* may have provided a model for the oscillations of Brachiano's and Vittoria's love affair in IV.ii, and *Othello* perhaps suggested the idea of Francisco's disguise as the war-like Moor, Mulinassar, in the last act, which, as one might expect, appears in none of the historical sources. In general it is undeniable that the tradition of revenge drama as it developed from Kyd's *The Spanish Tragedy* (*c.* 1590), particularly in its more recent forms as exemplified by Marston's *The Malcontent* (1604), *The Revenger's Tragedy* (1607), provided Webster with techniques of characterization and plot development with which to shape and fill out the outline of Brachiano and Vittoria's story, though it is harder here to be specific. Jonson, Marston, Middleton and Chapman all supplied one or two verbal details, but Webster's most traceable debt to contemporary drama other than Shakespeare is to the long-forgotten classical tragedies of Sir William Alexander, from which he took a large number of one- or two-line sententious utterances. There were two other main sources for sententious utterances, George Pettie's translation of Stefano Guazza's conduct book, *Civil Conversation* (translated in 1581), which Webster seems almost to have had open beside him when writing V.i, so frequent are his references to it, and Florio's translation of Montaigne's *Essays* (1603), also a favourite source for *The Duchess of Malfi*. Montaigne's clear-eyed, rather wry view of the world particularly leaves its mark on Flamineo's cynical asides in I.ii. He is the source for Flamineo's famous image of the summer bird-cage, and Webster's handling of this passage demonstrates his economical skill in transforming the phrasing of his source-material into something whose poetic quality is peculiarly his own. Flamineo, describing the irrational compulsions of amorous desire, says

'Tis just like a summer bird-cage in a garden: the birds that are without, despair to get in, and the birds that are within despair and are in a consumption for fear they shall never get out.

(I.ii.44–7)

The equivalent passage in Florio's Montaigne, on the subject of marriage, goes as follows:

It may be compared to a cage, the birds without dispaire to get in, and those within dispaire to get out.

(*Essays* III.v)

Webster retains Montaigne's sense but expands his image with a few words that change the rather colourless wording of the original into something intensely poignant and expressive of human absurdity. By making the cage 'a summer bird-cage in a garden' he implies the idea of love as both alluringly beautiful and transitory; by adding the phrase which elaborates on the despair of the birds inside the cage which 'are in a consumption for fear they shall never get out', he draws attention to the plight of the trapped creatures, which connects with his use elsewhere in the play (for instance in Cornelia's mad scene) of images of small birds to exemplify human misery and vulnerability.

Webster may have borrowed extensively and often at times very closely from other writers in the process of composition, perhaps, as has sometimes been suggested, working with a commonplace book at his side in which were recorded all the impressive phrases he had come across in his varied reading, but there is nothing slavish about such borrowing in *The White Devil*. What he brought to the story of Brachiano and Vittoria was not just a matter of revenge-tragedy background and motifs culled from contemporary drama, decorated with sententiae from Montaigne and others, and provided with touches of Italianate authenticity from a few tales and pamphlets, but a dramatist's imagination and powers of construction. By developing the characters of Flamineo and Francisco as he has done, Webster transformed his source material out of all recognition. The brooding, malcontent presence of the former, to whom so much commentary on the main action is given, is a vital factor in shaping the audience's perception of the other characters; and the inner changes he undergoes in the last act (perhaps 'spiritual' is not too strong a word for them) contribute importantly to any statement the play has to make about the significance of the lives and deaths of its characters. Francisco, whose role in the version of events known to Webster is far from clearly defined, becomes in the play the chief revenger, and his plots and strategies, particularly in the latter half, direct the action to its conclusion and constitute a distinctive comment on the revenge ethic. By various means Webster modifies and augments the dramatis personae of the story so as to prepare for the shaping of a random sequence of events into a plot: Vittoria's husband is transformed from a young to an old man; Cornelia and Marcello are made into critics of the morality of Vittoria and Brachiano; Zanche is added; Lodovico's motives for be-coming involved in the plot – his banishment and his passion for Isabella – are invented. The great majority of the scenes are invented, or at any rate do not originate in any known contemporary account of these events; the only detailed resemblance comes in Vittoria's death scene in V.vi, but even here the connection between Webster's play and con-temporary descriptions of Vittoria facing her death with 'religious-seem-ing boldness', as J. R. Brown in his introduction to the Revels edition of the play calls it, is momentary, and the ideas for the greater part of the scene belong entirely to the dramatist. While Webster clearly draws on established dramatic stereotypes for certain of his characters, for instance making Camillo into a version of the foolish old cuckold figure, Giovanni into the innocent and victimized child, Zanche into the morally loose but ultimately faithful maidservant, he creates for others a complexity and multifariousness which, despite their obvious staginess, give the action of the play at crucial moments the illusion of life. Flamineo and Vittoria in particular, though they could not have existed in the forms they have without the traditional patterns of characterization derived from the Kydian line of drama, are much more than just Webster's versions of stock figures; their changeableness, their apparent ability to respond to new situations, the way they themselves appear different according to the perspective from which they are seen, all these features are evidence of the power of Webster's dramatic imagination to organize and transform the raw material of his story, combining it with hints and details and background information from a clutch of different sources into a unique vision of life.

3. Plot Summary

Although the first section of *The White Devil* does not divide the play
into acts and scenes, most modern editors follow the divisions set up by
Sampson in his edition of 1904 without disagreement, so that it is reason-
able to use them in making a summary of the plot, even if it is not
absolutely certain they are what Webster intended. The scenes themselves
are very clearly demarcated, as one would expect with a dramatist who
up to this time had always worked in collaboration.

    I.i. In a short introductory scene set in Rome Count Lodovico receives
from his friends Antonelli and Gasparo the news that he has been
banished from Rome for a number of crimes against the state. Though
Antonelli and Gasparo consider the punishment just, Lodovico is bitterly
resentful, feeling that he has done no worse than many others, such as
the Duke of Brachiano, who got off scot-free, and he vows revenge
should he ever return.

    I.ii is a long scene set in the house of Camillo and Vittoria in which
the protagonists of the play are introduced and the main situation established. Brachiano, a rich and powerful figure in the state, has fallen in
love with Vittoria Corombona, a brilliant and beautiful gentlewoman,
married to the elderly fool Camillo. Vittoria's brother Flamineo, who
acts as Brachiano's secretary, agrees to help his employer win Vittoria in
the hope of ensuring his own social advancement. He contrives a trick to
get Camillo out of the way so that Brachiano can declare his love for
Vittoria, but Cornelia, mother to Vittoria and Flamineo, is also present,
overhears the love-scene and steps forward to upbraid the lovers for
their behaviour. Left alone at the end with his mother, Flamineo chal-
lenges her, angry that she has upset his scheming. He recognizes that he
has embarked on a crooked and dangerous course of action, but intends
nonetheless to pursue it.

    II.i. Isabella, Brachiano's wife, arrives in Rome with their young
son, and the setting is now Brachiano's palace. She has heard of her husband's pursuit of Vittoria, but is confident of her own ability to
win him back. The two most significant representatives in the play of
state power, Francisco de Medici, Duke of Florence, Isabella's brother,
and Cardinal Monticelso, cousin to Camillo, involve themselves in the
affair, urging Brachiano to consider the risks to his reputation and the
poor example set to his son in becoming known as Vittoria's lover. They
leave Brachiano with Isabella, expecting the couple to become reconciled,
but instead Brachiano casts his wife off, vowing never to sleep with her
again. However, when the Duke and the Cardinal return to the scene,

the selfless Isabella, hoping not to widen the breach between Brachiano and these potentates any further, pretends that it is she who has rejected her husband, and not the other way round. Camillo enters, and Flamineo plots with Brachiano to contrive his death the same night. Monticelso arranges a commission for Camillo in the army, and at the end of the scene reveals privately to Francisco that he wants above all to expose Brachiano's wrongdoing and to be revenged on him.

II.ii. The action of this scene takes place on the same night. Two dumbshows, instigated by a conjurer, are performed before Brachiano. In the first, Isabella is seen to die as she kisses a portrait of Brachiano which has been poisoned. In the second, Flamineo exercises with Camillo at a vaulting-horse, and in doing so contrives to break his neck. Brachiano watches with interest and satisfaction.

III.i. Preparations are made by Francisco and Monticelso for the trial of Vittoria, accused of complicity in Camillo's murder. Flamineo and his brother Marcello are also under arrest; Marcello expresses horror at Flamineo's open admission that he has acted as Brachiano's pander in order to win preferment. Visiting ambassadors assemble to attend the trial, which follows at once, with no break in the action.

III.ii is another very long scene, and the heart of the play. It takes place in a courtroom in Rome, where Vittoria is publicly arraigned, ostensibly for her part in Camillo's murder, actually for her way of life. There is irony in the fact that Brachiano, the true instigator of the murder, is present for much of the trial as an uninvited spectator, and he chooses to make an ostentatious departure at a high point in the proceedings, leaving Vittoria to fend for herself. Vittoria is addressed first by a hired lawyer who tries to insist that the proceedings be conducted in Latin, and is then dismissed for his pomposity by Francisco, who is impatient to have the trial underway. Monticelso is Vittoria's chief accuser, although, as Vittoria aptly points out, the role is inappropriate to a Cardinal of the Church. She answers him back courageously and brilliantly with a wit that exposes the weakness of his case, and Brachiano intervenes on her behalf. Francisco eventually admits that nothing can be proved against Vittoria in relation to the murder, and urges Monticelso to proceed only on the charge of incontinence. It is obvious that the whole proceeding is rigged, and Vittoria is naturally angry when she is insultingly sentenced to a spell of confinement in a house of penitent whores. The injustice is the more obvious in that Flamineo, who has been present throughout, gets off scot-free. In a brief but important coda at the end of the scene news of Isabella's death is brought to Francisco, her brother, by Lodovico, returning unannounced from exile, and her little son Giovanni mourns for his mother with a childish sincerity that is in strong contrast to his father's attitude.

III.iii. This scene takes place immediately after the trial, and depicts various responses to it. Flamineo puts on a mad act, pretending to be distracted by Vittoria's disgrace, although his bitterness may be in part genuine for the loss of his ambitious prospects. In a riddling dialogue with Lodovico the two malcontents form a pact until it is announced that Francisco has obtained official pardon for Lodovico's crimes. Flamineo is outraged at this injustice, and Lodovico now feels free to insult Flamineo openly. Marcello forces his brother to leave before the scene turns to violence.

IV.i moves to a new phase of the action. Monticelso advises Francisco to proceed covertly against Isabella's murderers while Francisco pretends reluctance to contemplate revenge of any sort. He reveals in soliloquy, however, that he has plans with which he does not trust Monticelso. Monticelso then produces his 'black book'; a list of the names of many kinds of criminals currently active in Rome, from which Francisco decides to compile his own list of murderers. Left alone, he has a vision of Isabella's ghost, which gives impetus to his plans. He decides to procure Lodovico to act for him, and meanwhile sends a letter to Vittoria in her prison, pretending to be in love with her, so that it will fall into Brachiano's hands and cause dissention between them.

IV.ii. Just as Francisco intends, Brachiano intercepts his letter to Vittoria and is filled with rage, first against Flamineo, to whom the letter has been given, then against Vittoria. Vittoria at once recognizes what Francisco is up to, but it takes a stirring display of passion before she can convince Brachiano that she has not been unfaithful to him. The lovers are reconciled, and plan, with Flamineo's assistance, to steal Vittoria out of her prison in page's disguise and escape with her to Padua, making use of the confusion that has ensued in Rome on the death of the Pope as a cover for their plot.

IV.iii. At the conclusion of the Papal conclave, during which Lodovico is seen acting in an official capacity to supervise the return of the ambassadors from the election of the new Pope, it is announced, first, that Monticelso has been elected Pope, and second, that Vittoria has escaped from Rome. Monticelso appears in robes of state to pronounce sentence of excommunication on her and Brachiano. After Francisco has briefly confirmed with Lodovico the latter's willingness to act with him in revenge against Brachiano, Monticelso then urges Lodovico strongly to abandon the project. Lodovico, confused, having expected

Monticelso's support, is about to do so, when Francisco has him presented with a thousand crowns, pretending the money has been sent secretly by Monticelso. Lodovico, his mind now made up, resolves to proceed to the murder.

V.i. For the last act, the setting shifts to Brachiano's palace in Padua. There has been an interval in time, during which Vittoria and Brachiano have married, and this scene takes place immediately after the marriage, which Flamineo regards as his crowning achievement. Revels to celebrate the marriage are planned. Unknown to Flamineo and Brachiano, however, Francisco, Lodovico and two of their associates have infiltrated Brachiano's court in disguise to carry out the revenge. Ironically, Brachiano especially welcomes and honours Francisco, who is disguised as a Moorish mercenary soldier. A quarrel arises between Flamineo and his brother Marcello over Zanche, Vittoria's Moorish maid-servant, who is in love with Flamineo; both Marcello and Cornelia think that Flamineo is demeaning himself by encouraging Zanche. Cornelia strikes Zanche, and the maid-servant, insulted, transfers her affections to the disguised Francisco.

V.ii. Flamineo, pursuing the family quarrel from the previous scene, runs Marcello through with a sword in Cornelia's presence. Cornelia is grief-stricken, but when Brachiano, dressed for the jousting, enters and enquires into Marcello's death, she attempts to save Flamineo by lying. He realizes the truth and, in order to assert his power over Flamineo, grants him a pardon that must be renewed every evening. The scene ends with Lodovico, unseen, sprinkling poison into Brachiano's helmet.

V.iii is Brachiano's death-scene. As Brachiano is dying from the effects of the poisoned helmet he becomes delirious and hallucinates. Lodovico and one of his fellow-conspirators appear at his bedside disguised as monks, pretending to perform the last rites. Left alone with him, they reveal their true identities and torment him with curses and insults in his dying moments. Finally they strangle him. Vittoria is overcome with grief but Flamineo is chiefly concerned for the fact that Brachiano has died without ever giving him any tangible reward for his services. Francisco congratulates Lodovico on the success of their plot against Brachiano; the next stage of his intrigues gets underway when Zanche, having revealed to him exactly how Camillo and Isabella met their deaths, also discloses her own plan to rob Vittoria that night and escape from the court, taking Francisco with her.

V.iv. Prince Giovanni denies Flamineo access to his rooms in the palace. Cornelia, mad with grief, sings a mourning lament over Marcello's body. Flamineo, moved by the sight, feels remorse for his way of life. Brachiano's ghost appears to him, giving signs that his own death is imminent. Feeling that he now has nothing to lose, he decides to confront Vittoria and either force some reward from her or kill her.

V.v. Lodovico urges Francisco to opt out of the revenge for his own security, and leave the remainder of the action to him, since he has nothing more to lose.

V.vi. Flamineo comes upon Vittoria at her prayers and claims his reward for services done for Brachiano. She offers him only the curse of Cain, who also murdered his brother. He then tells her that he has made a vow to Brachiano that neither he nor Vittoria will outlive their lord more than four hours. Vittoria, desperately plotting in asides with Zanche to save herself, agrees to a suicide pact with Flamineo, using two cases of pistols bequeathed by Brachiano. Vittoria and Zanche shoot first, and as Flamineo seems to be dying, Vittoria admits that she has no intention of killing herself too. Flamineo then rises from the ground, revealing that the pistols were not loaded and that he has been testing his sister's fidelity. At this point, Lodovico and his confederates, in their disguise as monks, break in and then reveal their true identities. Flamineo and Vittoria, recognizing that there is no escape, stand up boldly to their killers. Vittoria is stabbed first and then Flamineo. At the end of the scene Prince Giovanni and the ambassadors enter to take control. Lodovico is shot and wounded, but none the less rejoices in the successful achievement of his revenge.

4. Structure

The plot of *The White Devil* is rambling and difficult to summarize without distortion. There are a large number of characters, much intrigue and contrivance, but the real problem is that all the main characters are to different degrees ambiguous and their roles in the structure of the drama hard to define. Not only are their motivations sometimes unclear and hard to interpret, but we cannot be sure in some cases whether they are heroes or villains. Vittoria is an adulteress, and seems also to be the agent to the murders of her husband and her lover's wife; but she is not presented as a villain, and on some occasions the situations in which she appears seem to invite our sympathy for her, as for instance in the trial scene where she defends herself so spiritedly against the biased and unfair attacks of Monticelso and Francisco, and in IV.i where Brachiano, deceived by a lying letter planted by Francisco, violently accuses her of betraying him. Brachiano too is an ambiguous character morally and also in terms of his place in the play's structure. He is in fact the initiator of the central action, when he falls in love with Vittoria and determines to make her his mistress, irrespective of all obstacles; but in the scenes in which he appears his significance is nearly always overshadowed by the brilliant presence of Vittoria or the undercutting wit of Flamineo.

It has been suggested that Webster altered his original plan for the play from one centring on Brachiano to one where Vittoria's life, especially its final phases, is elevated to equal importance. The title-page to the original quarto begins, 'THE WHITE DIVEL, OR, The Tragedy of *Paulo Giordano Vrsini*, Duke of *Brachiano* . . .' implying a clearer focus on Brachiano as tragic protagonist, but the title then continues, 'With The Life and Death of Vittoria Corombona the famous Venetian Curtizan'. The phrase describing Vittoria suggests that Webster wished to capitalize on the more sensational aspects of his story, since, as he knew, Vittoria did not come from Venice, although it was a city notorious to the Jacobeans for its prostitutes, and she was hardly, by most standards, a 'courtesan'. The expansion of Vittoria's part in the plot could account for the unusual length of the fifth act and of the play as a whole, as well as for its lack of a single, obviously central character.

However this may be, the moral ambiguity of Brachiano's character remains, in that, although his behaviour is that of a cruel, ruthless and immoral man, his feeling for Vittoria seems intended to be strong and genuine, and the audience must be moved in some way during his death scene, otherwise the tragic climax of the play will go for nothing. Difficulties of another sort are constituted by Monticelso and Francisco. Initially their function is the same, as aggrieved relatives of the two wronged spouses, Camillo and Isabella, who are in a position to use their considerable power within the state to gain redress against Brachiano and Vittoria. They are not strongly individualized, and they are functionaries rather than characters to whom the audience is invited to respond personally. Their behaviour in the trial scene inclines us against them, since it so obviously represents a misuse of power. Subsequently, their ways divide. Monticelso, once elected to the Papacy, undergoes a radical change of heart in his attitude towards the affair of Brachiano and Vittoria and counsels Lodovico unequivocally against taking revenge. He withdraws from the action completely at the end of Act IV, never to reappear. Whether we are to interpret this as a conversion to the Christian principle of 'Vengeance is mine; I will repay, saith the Lord' (Romans XII: 19) is not clear. Francisco's moral approval of the revenge continues undeterred, and he insists on active, personal involvement in the revenge until virtually the last moment, when Lodovico, after a previous attempt has failed, manages to persuade him to quit the city and leave it to him to settle the fates of Vittoria and Flamineo. Thus Francisco is the one revenger who gets off scot-free, and attention is drawn in the closing moments of the play to the fact that he has been not only the chief contriver but also the authority for the whole revenge when Lodovico, arrested by Prince Giovanni's guards, is questioned by Giovanni:

GIOVANNI: You bloody villains,
  By what authority have you committed
  This massacre?
LODOVICO: By thine.
GIOVANNI: Mine?
LODOVICO: Yes, thy uncle,
  Which is a part of thee enjoin'd us to't:
  Thou know'st me I am sure, I am Count Lodowick,
  And thy most noble uncle in disguise
  Was last night in thy court.

(V.vi.280–7)

Lodovico himself is a character whose importance is difficult to assess. He begins and ends the play, and also has a vital part in the plot in the second half, returning uninvited from banishment to involve himself in the revenge on behalf of the family of Isabella, whom he claims to have loved, and also out of resentment against Brachiano. Again, he is a functionary rather than a character, a conventionally bitter, Elizabethan-style revenger, like Vendice in *The Revenger's Tragedy*, whose main motive for his dangerous and ultimately fatal commitment to the revenge seems to be an aesthetic pleasure in contrivance:

        I do glory yet
    That I can call this act mine own. For my part,
    The rack, the gallows, and the torturing wheel
    Shall be but sound sleeps to me; here's my rest:
    I limb'd this night-piece and it was my best.

(V.vi.291–5)

Despite the intense focus on him both at the beginning of the play, which opens so forcefully with his bitter exclamation, 'Banish'd?', and at the end, Lodovico is only intermittently interesting and the outlines of his character are never filled in.

Webster has often been criticized on account of *The White Devil*'s structure but, despite the difficulties outlined, there are many features of the play which suggest that he was concerned to achieve structural unity and coherence, even if the plot did not centre on a single protagonist. Plot is only one of the elements relevant to a consideration of structure in a play; the parts may be seen to be significantly related to one another by means of various kinds of pattern, by the repetition of incidents or events of a particular kind, for instance, like the series of ironic reversals in *The Revenger's Tragedy*, or the interlocking revenge actions in *The Spanish Tragedy*, by the recurrence of certain concepts or motifs in the language of the play, often linked with the same motifs in the action, as in the uses of storm, disguise or madness in *King Lear*, or by the duplication of functions and relationships between characters or groups of characters; for instance in *Hamlet* we can see that one of the ways in which the main plot of the play is related to the sub-plot is that each centres on a family group, and within these groups are two sets of fathers and sons, and that Hamlet's role as revenger of his father's death must make us reflect on Laertes, when he comes to play a similar role for Polonius.

One of the clearest patterns of action in *The White Devil* is that of rising and falling, when a character or faction achieves temporary success and then is cast down, often in counterpoint to the action of an opponent. If we consider the main characters to be divided into two groups, the Brachiano faction (chiefly Brachiano, Vittoria, Flamineo and, initially, Zanche) and the Francisco faction (Francisco and Monticelso, Lodovico, and those conspirators in Francisco's pay), we can perceive a kind of zigzag pattern in their progress.

At the beginning of the play, the fortunes of Brachiano and Vittoria are in the ascendant, as the plot contrived by Flamineo to establish their liaison proceeds successfully; the Francisco faction, on the other hand, are in decline, with the banishment of Lodovico, and this tendency culminates in the murders of Camillo and Isabella, which represents of course a corresponding high point for Brachiano and Vittoria. After the crisis point at the end of Act II, the relative positions of the two factions are progressively reversed; the trial and commitment of Vittoria to the house of convertites is a blow to the hopes of her party and a mark of success for her opponents, and Francisco's contrivance in bringing about a quarrel between Brachiano and Vittoria further contributes to his rise. The banishment of Brachiano and Vittoria by Monticelso, now Pope, at the end of Act IV, seems to confirm their downfall, but there is a brief reversal at the beginning of Act V when Flamineo announces:

> In all the weary minutes of my life,
> Day ne'er broke up till now. This marriage
> Confirms me happy.

(V.i.1–3)

But from this point on the Brachiano faction sinks into an irreversible decline: the infiltration of Francisco into Brachiano's court, the desertion of Zanche to the other side, and the fatal discord between Flamineo and Marcello are successive steps in their downfall.

Brachiano's death is followed by those of Vittoria and Flamineo; though Lodovico is captured he rejoices in the successful completion of his action. Francisco, the master-plotter, though not physically present, is not forgotten at the end. Giovanni's promise of retribution to come – 'All that have hands in this, shall taste our justice, / As I hope heaven' – seems no more than an empty gesture against him; his absence from the holocaust implies successful escape.

On a smaller scale, the pattern of alternate rising and falling can also be perceived as a structural feature within a single scene. The play's larger preoccupation with the fluctuations of fortune prepares us for the extraordinary oscillations in the final scene, where the Brachiano faction is now divided against itself, and Flamineo and Vittoria, previously allies, are antagonists. The scene opens with Flamineo challenging Vittoria, apparently at her prayers, to reward his services to the dead Brachiano. He establishes ascendancy first by means of surprise; promising to show her 'two case of jewels' left to him by Brachiano, he produces instead two cases of pistols. Vittoria, however, though acting out the part of the defenceless woman – 'What do you want? What would you have me do?' – is soon contriving to save herself, and regains the position of power over Flamineo with a trick, aided by the cooperation of Zanche. The women make a suicide pact with Flamineo, boldly appearing to assert their readiness for death; they are first to shoot him, and then each other, 'most religiously' swearing not to outlive him. But of course, once Flamineo has fallen, the women reveal that they have no intention at all of following suit. For a moment it seems that Flamineo has been the agent of his own downfall, outwitted by women. But Vittoria's triumph is only momentary; in the most unexpected change of fortune so far, just as Zanche is planning to make it appear that Flamineo has killed himself, he gets up, unwounded, revealing that the pistols have only shot blanks. Now brother and sister face each other on equal terms, the truth of their matching egoism revealed. Just as the balance is about to shift again, when Flamineo produces two more pistols (l. 165), the whole situation changes completely, as representatives of Francisco's faction, led by Lodovico, appear on the scene, to enact the last stage of the revenge, and Flamineo and Vittoria reunite for the last time, facing death together.

The series of rising and falling actions in the play, the alternation of success and failure, the vying for pre-eminence between factions and individuals, constitute the play's most noticeable structural feature. There are also other kinds of repetition which suggests that Webster allowed for connections to be made between different parts of the play. Two ghosts of the murdered appear, each to a single, specially selected individual: Isabella's to Francisco in IV.i, Brachiano's to Flamineo in V.iv; each prompts the man who sees it to some definitive, ultimately fatal, action. Two of the characters go mad, Brachiano in V.iii, owing to the effects of his poisoned helmet, Cornelia in V.iv, from grief at the death of Marcello. Each has hallucinations of animals and of death. These striking repetitions of a sensational kind of event lend a certain formalism to the play's structure, especially in its later stages, suggesting that however chaotic and meaningless life may seem to individuals – as Brachiano, Vittoria and Flamineo all imply in their dying moments – there is a shape and pattern to it seen from a larger perspective. There are many other sorts of echoes and repetitions in the play, which have implications both for its structure and its thematic content. The device of a scene played between two or more characters while another commentates on it, either from the sidelines, or unseen and in asides, is used at two important points. In I.ii, for example, the encounter of Vittoria and Brachiano is witnessed by Zanche and Flamineo from one point of view, approving the action, and by Cornelia, who lurks, unseen by the other participants until she reveals herself towards the end, from another. In IV.ii, Flamineo is again the commentator on a scene played between Vittoria and Brachiano, his detached presence and wryly cool asides counterpointing the lovers' passionate involvement. The effect is somewhat similar in II.ii, when Brachiano is a witness to the two murders in dumbshow, first of Isabella, then of Camillo, and remarks approvingly in each case upon the action: 'Excellent, then she's dead,' 'Twas quaintly done.' In V.iii the structure and organization of the triangular scene between the disguised Francisco, Zanche and Lodovico is clearly designed to echo and recall earlier scenes between Brachiano, Vittoria and Flamineo. Here Lodovico takes on the same role as Flamineo, a cynical commentator standing aside to witness an intimate encounter between the other characters, with distancing remarks addressed to the audience, such as, 'Mark her I prithee, she simpers like the suds / A collier hath been wash'd in' (ll. 242–3). Just as Vittoria wooed Brachiano with an account of a dream she wishes him to fulfil (II.i) so Zanche courts Francisco with a dream of her own, appropriately much more obvious and unequivocal in application than Vittoria's. Where the first scene acts as direct prelude to the murders of Isabella and Camillo, so the second leads up to the revelation, from Zanche to Francisco, of exactly how these murders were performed. The connection between the two scenes, one early in the action, the other near the play's conclusion, implies a neatness and circularity in the structure of events.

The situation of a triangular confrontation whereby one character defends him- or herself against the accusations or onslaught of two opponents is repeated many times over: for example, in I.i Lodovico justifies his rage at being banished, against the consolations offered by Gasparo and Antonelli; in II.i Brachiano outfaces accusations of immorality by Francisco and Monticelso, as Vittoria does similarly in III.ii; he is impotent, however, against the orchestrated torments of Gasparo and Lodovico in V.iii.

The use of recurrent motifs in the language of the play is so important a device in *The White Devil* that it will be dealt with separately (see Imagery and Dramatic Language). If repeated patterns of events are not necessarily obvious until one looks a little way beneath the play's surface, there is no doubt that the repeated use of certain images is evident even to the least perceptive reader or audience. Images of animals, for example, of poison and disease, of devils, and of light and dark lend brilliance to the language in every scene. The tragic power of Webster's poetry has always been admired, and the conspicuous recurrence of vivid images drawing on linked and interconnected ideas does much to give the play coherence.

The duplication of character-groupings has already been touched upon in the account of the rivalry between the factions of Francisco and Brachiano. Each of these Dukes is an important secular leader, head of a powerful house. The political situation of Renaissance Italy, which was of course not a unified country but a collection of independent and warring city-states, lent itself to the depiction of a society governed by rivalry and competition for power on a large scale and at the highest level, such as would not be as appropriate for an image of a country like England, ruled by a constitutional monarch. As Francisco has his large household of dependents and menials, so too has Brachiano. Lodovico is a tool-villain for Francisco, as Flamineo is for Brachiano. Each potentate rules a small empire and personally deals out rewards and punishments, irrespective of the claims of law. When Brachiano cuts off Isabella in Vittoria's favour he deals a mortal insult to Isabella's family, which naturally her brother Francisco must avenge. The rivalry of these two power figures is at the heart of the play. But there are also other instances of doubling, significant on a smaller scale. As there are two

Dukes and two rival centres of power, so there are two sets of married couples, Vittoria and Camillo, Brachiano and Isabella, two adulterous lovers, two wronged spouses. The liaison is opposed on two fronts, from outside by the families of the wronged spouses, and from within by Vittoria's mother Cornelia. Cornelia's opposition is counterbalanced by the approval of Flamineo, who does all he can to further the arrangement in the interests of his own career. The liaison of Vittoria and Brachiano is echoed on another level by that between Zanche and Flamineo. Francisco, the arch-intriguer, plays a similar part in each relationship, attempting to come between Vittoria and Brachiano in IV.i by means of the false love-letter, and luring Zanche away from Flamineo in Act V in his Moorish disguise.

Looked at in this way, the play can be seen as a complex network of interrelationships. This is not to say that the criticisms of Webster's powers of construction, mentioned earlier, are entirely without foundation, for the play undeniably has its loose ends; and compared with a really tight structure, such as that of *The Revenger's Tragedy*, for instance, or Jonson's *The Alchemist*, Webster's plotting is loose and sometimes opportunistic. He is quite prepared to sacrifice internal consistency or neatness for the sake of local effects. But nonetheless, as has been suggested, the patterning in the play has a moral as well as an aesthetic purpose, and contributes significantly to the formulation of a view of life.

5. Imagery and Dramatic Language

Much has been written about the imagery in Webster's plays, since it is both brilliantly conspicuous and very profuse. The power of Webster's tragic poetry, so admired by the poet Swinburne, which caused many nineteenth-century writers and theatre critics to rank Webster next to Shakespeare and Marlowe in their hierarchy of Elizabethan playwrights, is due in large part to his imagery. It has been calculated that there are more than five hundred images each in *The White Devil* and *The Duchess of Malfi* (images in the sense used by Ralph Berry, in *The Art of John Webster*, p. 59, of 'language whose purpose is other than a literal statement of fact: whose aim is to evoke associations over and above the needs of narrative action'), in comparison with a total of three hundred and ninety-nine for *Troilus and Cressida*, Shakespeare's play with the highest total. Every scene, every major speech of each play is full of them; they are used by every character. In the first twelve lines of *The White Devil*, four images, all of them to have significance throughout the play, appear:

>   gods
>   That govern the whole world! Courtly reward,
>   And punishment! Fortune's a right whore.
>
>   Your wolf no longer seems to be a wolf
>   Than when she's hungry.
>
>   The violent thunder is adored by those
>   Are pash'd in pieces by it.
>
>   (I.i.2–4, 8–9, 11–12)

This distribution is typical of the style of the whole play, and so too is the vividness and quality of passionate feeling which the images impart to the sentiments expressed. Webster's favourite areas of subject-matter, those which are most frequently used to function, in the term used by I. A. Richards, as the vehicles of his images, are animals, poison and disease, the law, storms and weather, light and darkness, diamonds and other bright jewels, devils and witches. The reader familiar with Webster's dramatic language may feel that these topics are inherently poetically suggestive, almost irrespective of the way they are referred to. But it is not just the subject-matter of Webster's images that is significant but the way in which it is used. The interconnectedness of the imagery is especially important, the relation of images one to another which helps to build up a complex of meaning and associations deriving from the repeated usage and from the contexts of these usages. When, for instance, Flamineo says in his dying moments:

>   'Tis well yet there's some goodness in my death,
>   My life was a black charnel. I have caught
>   An everlasting cold
>
>   (V.vi.267–9)

the lines are powerfully effective in several ways on account of their relation to certain image-patterns in the play to which they come as a culmination. There have been many earlier references to graves and charnel-houses, and to the closeness of life to death, most particularly in V.iv, when the mad Cornelia sings a dirge over Marcello's corpse, and afterwards the ghost of Brachiano appears to Flamineo and throws earth upon him out of a pot of lily-flowers containing a skull. 'Black' is of course an appropriate word for a charnel or burial place, but it is also the last of many references to black and its associations with sin and death, as in the mourning black of Giovanni (III.ii.309), the 'black lust' of Vittoria (III.i.7), the 'black book' of criminals compiled by Monticelso (IV.i.33), and the 'black lake' (V.ii.83) into which Brachiano will fall after death. Black is the only colour-word other than white in the play. The 'everlasting cold', which signifies Flamineo's death, is a marvellously resonant phrase, rendering the mundane unexpected and macabre, juxtaposing the temporary and the eternal. Perhaps no play ever contained so many and varied references to disease as *The White Devil*; from vomiting and jaundice to ulcers, abscesses and syphilis, the language is preoccupied with this way of expressing moral corruption. Flamineo's common cold is the most common-place of all conditions of ill-health, but in his case it is fatal. The phrase perfectly suits his characteristic manner of offhand cynicism.

By means of such a network of associations as this, the imagery of *The White Devil* is an important contribution to the structural cohesion of the play. This is especially the case with the images deriving from the title, which develop the central and over-riding idea of the discrepancy between appearance and reality. One thinks first, perhaps, of the images used by other characters to express their feelings about Vittoria, such as Brachiano's 'the devil in crystal' (IV.ii.88), Monticelso's 'Poison'd perfumes' (III.ii.81), 'apples' of Sodom which turn to 'soot and ashes' at the touch (III.ii.64–7), 'shipwrecks in calmest weather' and counterfeit jewels, which all emphasize her deceptive allure and the way it masks her moral evil. The theme is more generally referred to in several ways. Lodovico, for instance, deceived by Francisco in IV.iii into thinking that the Pope has secretly sent him money to pursue revenge against Brachiano, generalizes about the deceptive behaviour of great men:

> O the art,
> The modest form of greatness! that do sit
> Like brides at wedding dinners, with their looks turn'd
> From the least wanton jests, their puling stomach
> Sick of the modesty, when their thoughts are loose,
> Even acting of those hot and lustful sports
> Are to ensue about midnight: such is his cunning!
>
> (IV.iii.142–8)

This is a characteristically cynical image to express the hypocrisy of human nature, implicitly relating the Pope's appearance of virtue to the pretended modesty of a bride. Francisco also expresses this view of human activity as deceptive, never as grand, virtuous or significant as it appears:

As ships seem very great upon the river, which show very little upon the seas: so some men i'th' court seem Colossuses in a chamber, who if they came into the field would appear pitiful pigmies.

(V.i.118–21)

39

As Flamineo tells Camillo, the organs of perception are in themselves fallible; one sees what one is disposed to see, not what is actually there:

> they that have the yellow jaundice, think all objects they look on to be yellow. Jealousy is worser, her fits present to a man, like so many bubbles in a basin of water, twenty several crabbed faces; many times makes his own shadow his cuckold-maker.

> (I.ii.109–13)

But it is not only individuals who behave deceptively or see mistakenly; life itself is inherently deceptive:

> Glories, like glow-worms, afar off shine bright
> But look'd to near, have neither heat nor light.

> (V.i.41–2)

> *Prosperity doth bewitch men seeming clear,*
> *But seas do laugh, show white, when rocks are near.*

> (V.vi.248–9)

Other major kinds of imagery reinforce several of these views of human life. The play is full of references to animals, many of which imply there is little distinction between human and animal behaviour, even at its grossest and most bestial. Dogs and wolves are mentioned more than any others: great men, says Lodovico, are like wolves, voracious when hungry but otherwise able to conceal their appetites. Dog and wolf imagery is particularly applied by men to women, in reference to their sexual behaviour. Flamineo says women 'are like curs'd dogs, civility keeps them tied all daytime, but they are let loose at midnight' (I.ii.197–9); Brachiano, enraged with Vittoria, claims that 'Woman to man / Is either a god or a wolf' (IV.ii.91–2). Flamineo, asked his opinion of 'perfum'd gallants', that is, court rakes, answers in his cynical way,

> They have a certain spice of the disease.
> For they that sleep with dogs, shall rise with fleas.

> (V.i.169–70)

When he is pretending to be dying from Vittoria and Zanche's bullets he says he has been 'Kill'd with a couple of braches'. Vittoria, too, uses this comparison for the behaviour of Monticelso and Francisco during her trial. 'The wolf may prey the better,' she says, when Brachiano departs from the court, leaving her to defend herself. The lesser men are likened to dogs rather than wolves; Brachiano insultingly calls Flamineo his 'blood-hound' (IV.ii.51), and Monticelso addresses Lodovico in the same spirit:

> Wretched creature!
> I know that thou art fashion'd for all ill,
> Like dogs, that once get blood, they'll ever kill.
>
> (IV.iii.101–103)

It is one of the vilest insults that the dying Brachiano's tormentors give him, that he will 'stink / Like a dead fly-blown dog' (V.iii.167–8).

Animal imagery is always used to demean and belittle, so that it is not surprising to find it frequently applied to one of the most ridiculed characters in the play, Camillo. He is 'an ass in's foot-cloth' (I.ii.52), a capon, a maggot in white satin, a silkworm, a hornless stag, and 'a head fill'd with calves' brains without any sage in them' (I.ii.135); his house is a dovecote, preyed on by polecats. Most of these images occur in the speech of Flamineo, one of the chief belittlers in the play, and they help to characterize the quality of his observations on life, which are generally bitter. From time to time, however, his animal references take on another tone:

I myself have loved a lady and pursued her with a great deal of under-age protestation, whom some three or four gallants that have enjoyed would with all their hearts have been glad to have been rid of. 'Tis just like a summer bird-cage in a garden: the birds that are without, despair to get in, and the birds that are within despair and are in a consumption for fear they shall never get out.

> (I.ii.41–7)

This is the same disenchantment as before, but the ways in which Webster changes this image, which, as we have seen, is derived from Montaigne's *Essays*, suggest that he was aiming for an effect of pathos not to be found in other animal references. In particular, Webster makes the image less specific than in Montaigne, where it applied to marriage, so that here it applies partly to love but also more generally to the perversity of human desire; and he adds the adjective 'summer' to the bird-cage, lending connotations of transience and brief seasonal appetite. The image occurs again near the end of the play, when Flamineo, moved by Cornelia's madness, feels that 'strange thing . . . Compassion' within himself, and reflects back over his life:

> I have liv'd
> Riotously ill, like some that live in court.
> And sometimes, when my face was full of smiles
> Have felt the maze of conscience in my breast.
> Oft gay and honour'd robes those tortures try,
> *We think cag'd birds sing, when indeed they cry.*
>
> (V.iv.117–22)

Other birds and small creatures are mentioned by Cornelia, earlier in this scene, especially in her beautiful lament for Marcello:

> *Call for the robin red breast and the wren,*
> *Since o'er shady groves they hover,*
> *And with leaves and flow'rs do cover*
> *The friendless bodies of unburied men.*
> *Call unto his funeral dole*
> *The ant, the field-mouse, and the mole*
> *To rear him hillocks, that shall keep him warm*
> *And (when gay tombs are robb'd) sustain no harm,*
> *But keep the wolf far thence: that's foe to men,*
> *For with his nails he'll dig them up again.*

(V.iv.94–103)

Here these little creatures are imagined as friendly to mankind, in their small way, and capable of acts of kindness such as human beings cannot or do not perform. The effect of Cornelia's dirge is to emphasize human loneliness and isolation.

The feeling for animal life displayed here is reminiscent of that in the various animal fables and in the proverbial lore of animals that Webster uses as vehicles for moralizing in both his tragedies. When Monticelso advises Francisco to bide his time before taking revenge he uses a series of animal comparisons:

> Bear your wrongs conceal'd,
> And, patient as the tortoise, let this camel
> Stalk o'er your back unbruis'd: sleep with the lion,
> And let this brood of secure foolish mice
> Play with your nostrils; till the time be ripe.

(IV.i.14–18)

Flamineo, wishing to bring home to Brachiano his desire to have his services recompensed, does so with an old story of the crocodile and the bird who ministers to it by extracting from its jaws the worms which cause toothache (IV.ii); he draws on traditional animal lore again in V.iv for an apt saying to illustrate the wise and tactful way to flatter those in power:

Wise was the courtly peacock, that being a great minion, and being compar'd for beauty, by some dottrels that stood by, to the kingly eagle, said the eagle was a far fairer bird than herself, not in respect of her feathers, but in respect of her long tallants.

(V.iv.5)

Imagery of this kind is recognizably traditional, and not peculiar to

Webster. That the Elizabethans clearly took pleasure in using proverbial lore and stock phrases is generally reflected in the drama of the period, and it is important for modern readers of Webster to understand that there was nothing secondhand or inferior to his audiences in the use of such language.

The imagery of prison and disease represents another pervasive strain of figurative expression relating both generally to the ubiquitous conception of corruption and decay, and more specifically to the relationship of Vittoria and Brachiano. The characters consistently see both themselves and each other operating like poisoners or poison, and the world they live in as diseased. Lodovico's influence over his former followers has been, says Gasparo, emetic:

> Your followers
> Have swallowed you like mummia, and being sick
> With such unnatural and horrid physic
> Vomit you up i'th' kennel –

> (I.v.15–18)

The idea of exotic medicines which can act like poison as well is also present in Flamineo's plot to destroy Monticelso and Francisco: 'I will compound a medicine out of their two heads, stronger than garlic, deadlier than stibium; the cantharides which are scarce seen to stick upon the flesh when they work to the heart, shall not do it with more silence or invisible cunning' (II.i.283–7). Poison acts invisibly, undetected, and can make use of the most incongruous or unexpected objects as its vehicle; for instance, the doctor whom Brachiano employs to poison Isabella can, says Flamineo, 'poison a kiss', and does so. The portrait of Brachiano which Isabella kisses at night is the instrument of her death, signifying how fatal to her has been her love for her husband. Poison and disease images also qualify the relationship between Brachiano and Vittoria, who is called a 'Poison'd perfume' by Monticelso, the epitome of all poison to be found in animals and minerals. Brachiano in anger imagines Vittoria infecting him with venereal disease:

> O, I could be mad,
> Prevent the curs'd disease she'll bring me to,
> And tear my hair off.

> (IV.ii.45)

'Prevent' here means foresee or anticipate, and Brachiano means that he will anticipate the effects of venereal disease by tearing out his own hair first. Later in the same scene Vittoria uses similar ideas to convey her sense of Brachiano's fatal influence on herself and her family:

> Thou hast stain'd the spotless honour of my house,
> And frightened thence noble society:
> Like those, which sick o'th' palsy, and retain
> Ill-scenting foxes 'bout them, are still shunn'd
> By those of choicer nostrils . . .
> I had a limb corrupted to an ulcer,
> But I have cut it off: and now I'll go
> Weeping to heaven on crutches.

(IV.ii.108–12, 121–3)

Brachiano's reputation is poisoned by his association with Vittoria, as he is literally poisoned by Lodovico. It is of course an additional irony that the poison is sprinkled in his beaver, the face-guard of his helmet, which he dons for protection in the jousting. When Vittoria comes to his death-bed to comfort him, his words to her bear both literal and ironic meanings: 'Do not kiss me, for I shall poison thee.'

The poison and disease imagery is also used more generally in the play. Cornelia's image of Camillo's household as a poisoned garden (I.ii) picks up connotations of deathly and diseased growth from Vittoria's account to Brachiano of her dream, a few lines earlier, with its references to the yew-tree growing in a graveyard to be supplanted by 'a withered blackthorn'. Camillo himself, whose lack of vitality is suggested in this image, is like a gilder whose brain has decayed through the inhaling of poisonous fumes of quicksilver (I.ii.28), balding from disease and sexually incapable. Decay and corruption emanate from his household; no act, no relationship, in the world of this play is free from taint. Isabella hopes her love for Brachiano will 'charm his poison' and 'keep him chaste from an infected straying' (II.i.17–18) but to no avail, and she herself dies by poison; the apparently beautiful and brilliant Vittoria is a 'disease' to Brachiano; Flamineo thrives under Brachiano's protection 'like a wolf [ulcer] in a woman's breast' (V.iii.56). The desire for wealth and power at the heart of the play, which motivates so much of the intrigue, acts itself like poison: 'There's nothing so holy but money will corrupt and putrify it' (III.iii.26), as Flamineo says. It is fitting, then, that death comes as a cure; Flamineo says, displaying his pistols,

> These are two cupping-glasses, that shall draw
> All my infected blood out.

(V.vi.102–103)

Ideas of disturbance and inversion in the natural order implied by these images (life as sickness, death as cure, love as poison and so on) are echoed in references to cosmic disorder, such as storms, earthquakes and the appearance of comets and other supernatural portents. Cornelia's curse on Vittoria in I.ii is said to raise 'a fearful and prodigious storm', and the anger of Isabella's family against Brachiano sounds thunderbolts (II.i); Lodovico's revenge 'threat[s] A violent storm' (IV.iii.99) and causes an 'earthquake' (III.ii.134). Vittoria sees Flamineo's death as 'a blazing ominous star' (V.vi.130); the same image is applied twice to her, suggesting the startling and fatal power of her beauty.

There are several characteristic features of Webster's dramatic art to be discerned in his uses of imagery. In particular, critics have praised the 'resolute consistency' with which he 'elaborates an extended sequence of diverse but interrelated images' (H. T. Prince, 'The Function of Imagery in Webster', p. 718) and the fusion of 'figure in action and figure in language', as for instance in the images of poison just discussed. While such uses of imagery are familiar to us from Shakespeare's plays it should not be supposed that they are common in the work of all the dramatists of this period. Imagery also plays an important part in the creation of several kinds of witty effect, without which the dialogue of *The White Devil* would lack an important source of sustenance. The speech of Flamineo in particular is characterized by certain uses of imagery. He talks at one point about his 'court wisdom', which seems to refer to cynical generalizations and aphoristic expressions of the type he then exemplifies: 'To reprehend princes is dangerous: and to over-commend some of them is palpable lying' (V.iii.69–70). He has a range of expressions of this kind, mostly reliant for their effect (unlike this one) on the striking quality of the images he uses: the 'summer bird-cage' image of I.ii is a good example, demonstrating both the qualities of generalization from specific example, disenchantment in the view of human contrariousness and the vivid life of the image itself. His remarks about great men's promises (V.i.135) and about flatterers (V.iii.45) also illustrate these qualities. So pronounced is his tendency to generalization that some of his speeches, seen out of context, appear to consist of a series of unrelated aphorisms:

> Mark his penitence.
> Best natures do commit the grossest faults,
> When they're giv'n o'er to jealousy; as best wine
> Dying makes strongest vinegar. I'll tell you;
> The sea's more rough and raging than calm rivers,
> But nor so sweet nor wholesome. A quiet woman

> Is a still water under a great bridge.
> A man may shoot her safely.

(IV.ii.174–81)

His function in the play as mouthpiece or commentator is expressed in speeches of this kind, which are often signalled with some kind of self-conscious phrase like the reference to his own 'court wisdom' or 'I'll tell you' in this speech. He is to be seen as someone who plays the part of commentator, and announces that he is doing so. He is sometimes given generalizations and proverbial utterances which characterize him as a learned or bookish man; in I.ii he refers to an anecdote from Plutarch to justify to his mother his actions as pander for Brachiano:

> Lycurgus wond'red much men would provide
> Good stallions for their mares, and yet would suffer
> Their fair wives to be barren.

(I.ii.340–2)

At the end of IV.ii he tells Brachiano the traditional animal fable about the crocodile with toothache; Brachiano at once extracts the meaning:

> Your application is, I have not rewarded
> The service you have done me.

(IV.ii.234–5)

Flamineo unexpectedly denies this interpretation, and proposes another, whereby Vittoria instead is the crocodile in the story, and Brachiano the bird who relieves her of the worm; but in an aside to the audience he then appears to deny this counter-reading and to point out that the whole performance with the fable was a kind of role-playing:

> It may appear to some ridiculous
> Thus to talk knave and madman; and sometimes
> Come in with a dried sentence, stuff'd with sage.
> But this allows my varying of shapes.

(IV.ii.241–4)

The 'dried sentence', here meaning 'sententia' or convential moralized utterance, not only characterizes Flamineo's style in the play but also relates to the regular use of sententious couplets by many of the characters. The use of the rhymed couplet is of course a conventional device in Elizabethan drama, sometimes to mark the end of a scene or else to single out a particular part of a speech for notice as an utterance of general significance, with relevance outside its context. Webster uses the couplet in both these ways, but also, in keeping with the play's prevalent tone of questioning established values, sometimes places it within a speech in such a way that the sententious quality is parodied or mocked. When in II.i Flamineo answers Brachiano's enquiry as to how Camillo will be murdered with such a couplet, the effect is distinctly mocking:

BRACHIANO: But for Camillo?
FLAMINEO: He dies this night by such a politic strain,
            Men shall suppose him by's own engine slain.

(II.i.314–16)

Frequently the sentiment expressed in the couplet is so overtly cynical that the very conception of an utterance such as this being worth generalization is also mocked. Thus Lodovico concludes the first scene:

> Great men sell sheep, thus to be cut in pieces,
> When first they have shorn them bare and sold their fleeces.

And Francisco in soliloquy ends IV.i with a series of couplets interspersed with single unrhyming lines based mockingly on proverbial wisdom:

> He that deals all by strength, his wit is shallow:
> When a man's head goes through each limb will follow.
> The engine for my business, bold Count Lodowick;
> 'Tis gold must such an instrument procure,
> With empty fist no man doth falcons lure.
> Brachiano, I am now fit for thy encounter.
> Like the wild Irish I'll ne'er think thee dead,
> Till I can play at football with thy head.

(IV.i.131–8)

Cornelia and Marcello are among the few characters whose rhymed *sententiae* are used in the conventional way, without creating effects of mockery or parody. Marcello dies with a couplet which echoes his mother's theme of the destruction due to befall their family (V.ii.23–4) and Cornelia concludes the dirge for him with the proverbial lines

> His wealth is summ'd, and this is all his store:
> This poor men get; and great men get no more.

(V.iv.108–109)

The mocking wit of *The White Devil*'s dramatic language, conveyed through imagery and through uses of rhymed couplets, is also to be found in a certain style of dialogue, whereby two or more characters develop an exchange by means of play on a particular image. So when Camillo, excusing himself for not sleeping regularly with Vittoria, cites the example of a silkworm, which 'useth to fast every third day, and the next following spins the better', Vittoria cleverly twists the meaning of his image in her reply, 'you'll spin a fair thread, trust to't', using a proverbial phrase referring to a job badly done. A few lines later Flamineo comments as the gullible Camillo leaves the scene, 'Thou entanglest thyself in thine own work like a silkworm.' This device is a common feature of verbal duels in the play, where one character attempts to score off another by taking up and re-applying his own words. Brachiano and Francisco do it to one another several times in their heated encounter in II.i; Flamineo mocks his mother in I.ii.272 by this method; Vittoria scores off the lawyer hired to plead against her at her trial:

LAWYER: Well then have at you.
VITTORIA: I am at the mark sir, I'll give aim to you,
And tell you how near you shoot.

(III.ii.23–5)

The dramatic language of *The White Devil* loses none of its life or brilliance for a modern audience or reader from the knowledge that so much of it is borrowed from other literary sources. How Webster's contemporaries responded to his use of images or expressions already half-familiar to them we cannot know, for the usual reasons of historical distance but also because it is impossible to be certain how far Webster did expect his audience to recognize his borrowings. But it is clear that at key points in the play Webster relies heavily on his ability to use vivid imagery, sometimes borrowed, sometimes not, to create emotional effects, and that this ability never fails him. Brachiano, dying in agony, chills the heart when he contrasts his own fate with the peaceful departings of others:

> O thou soft natural death, that art joint-twin
> To sweetest slumber: no rough-bearded comet
> Stares on thy mild departure: the dull owl
> Beats not against thy casement: the hoarse wolf
> Scents not thy carrion. Pity winds thy corse,
> Whilst horror waits on princes.

(V.iii.30–5)

Death, the abnormal, and the supernatural were subjects that Webster handled with particular imaginative flair; Cornelia in her madness, Vittoria and Flamineo facing their murderers, these are situations which demand all his ability to produce evocative imagery. His language has striking powers of sinister suggestion; its eeriness is no better illustrated than in Flamineo's advice to dying men to put no faith in their wives:

> O men
> That lie upon your death-beds, and are haunted
> With howling wives, ne'er trust them; they'll remarry
> Ere the worm pierce your winding sheet; ere the spider
> Make a thin curtain for your epitaphs.
>
> (V.vi.152–6)

6. Themes

Revenge

The theme with which most modern readers or audiences would first associate *The White Devil* is revenge, and the opening scene of the play seems intended to encourage this idea, concerning as it does the resentment of an apparently villainous character, Lodovico, against powerful enemies who have brought about his banishment. His memorable threat of revenge – 'I'll make Italian cut-works in their guts/If ever I return' – seems placed so as to overshadow events to follow. This said, he disappears for some time from the action, and his involvement in revenge is delayed until the second half of the play. It soon becomes clear, however, that although revenge, of another sort, is to be central to the play, the revenge action and the roles of the various characters within it are not entirely conventionally organized in terms of the usual revenge structure. A double crime is committed, the murders of Camillo and Isabella, and the families of the victims take action against the perpetrators of the crime and eventually succeed in killing them. Brachiano and Vittoria are the villains, and, initially, Monticelso and Francisco the revengers. But though there are various virtuous characters, Cornelia, Isabella, Giovanni and Marcello, morally opposed to the behaviour of Brachiano and Vittoria, the flow of sympathy aroused by the play by no means goes against Brachiano and Vittoria, who, despite their evident culpability, emerge as more attractive characters than either the revengers or the virtuous. There is further modification to the revenge schema in that Monticelso in Act IV opts totally out, and is replaced as an active revenger by Lodovico, who, despite his indirect relationship to the victims of the crime (he claims to have lusted after Isabella), is the only one to see the revenge action fully completed. One of the most prominent characters in the play, Flamineo, is entirely subsidiary to the crime, although he is included in the final revenge and is in fact the last to die.

Revenge as a concept is introduced to the play twice before the main crimes take place, first by Lodovico who blames Vittoria and Brachiano for his banishment, and then by Monticelso, who takes Brachiano's cuckolding of Camillo as a slight to his family honour, being Camillo's cousin. For Monticelso, however, the chance of getting back at Brachiano, the leader of a rival power faction, is more important than requiting wrongs done to Camillo; he sends Camillo away on a naval commission, just so that his absence from Rome will give Brachiano the opportunity to consummate his affair with Vittoria, and there will be real cause to persecute him; he justifies his action rather boldly:

> It may be objected I am dishonourable,
> To play thus with my kinsman, but I answer,
> For my revenge I'd stake a brother's life,
> That being wrong'd durst not avenge himself.

(II.i.389–92)

The exact meaning of these lines is hard to come at; Monticelso is using Camillo as a pawn, but he also seems to be saying that he is so intent on revenge that he would be prepared to hazard the life of the kinsman on whose behalf he is taking the revenge.

But Camillo's death at the end of Act II, enacted in dumbshow, results not in Brachiano's arrest but in the trial of Vittoria. She is acquitted for lack of evidence on the charge of complicity in Camillo's death, but instead found guilty of incontinence, and in her turn vows vengeance on Monticelso and Francisco for the rigged trial and ignominious punishment.

A new phase of the action is initiated by the public announcement of Isabella's death at the end of the trial scene. Although her murder seems actually to have preceded Camillo's, Webster separates the two crimes, and delays the introduction of this more significant murder until after the trial. It is this specifically which motivates Francisco, Isabella's brother, to involve himself in revenge. At this point in the play the revenge action seems to assume a more conventional shape. The announcement of Isabella's death at the end of the long trial scene, with the sudden appearance of the boy Giovanni dressed in mourning clothes, and his pathetic memories of his mother's unhappiness –

> I have known her wake an hundred nights,
> When all the pillow, where she laid her head,
> Was brine-wet with her tears

– creates, if only momentarily, an unequivocal surge of sympathy for the grieving child and also for Francisco as the bereft brother. In the next scene Lodovico, whose imminent return from banishment has already been mentioned, reappears, his pardon obtained by Francisco, and in a brief but sinister passage with Flamineo, insults Vittoria and arouses Flamineo to strike him. This prepares for an alliance to be set up between Francisco and Lodovico against Brachiano and his faction, the chief of which is of course Flamineo. Francisco's gradual commitment to revenge is presented in IV.i in such a way as to make it clear that this is a very different kind of action, differently motivated, from Monticelso's efforts on his kinsman's behalf. Francisco seems initially reluctant to proceed against Brachiano, rather unexpectedly giving his responsibility as a prince to his subjects as the reason:

> Shall I defy him, and impose a war
> Most burthensome on my poor subjects' necks,
> Which at my will I have not power to end?
> You know; for all the murders, rapes, and thefts,
> Committed in the horrid lust of war,
> He that unjustly caus'd it first proceed,
> Shall find it in his grave and in his seed.
>
> (IV.i.5–11)

Monticelso has quite different ideas from this open and honourable course of action, and urges Francisco to the kind of covert procedures more characteristic of the revenger:

> Bear your wrongs conceal'd,
> And, patient as the tortoise, let this camel
> Stalk o'er your back unbruis'd ...
>   till the time be ripe
> For th' bloody audit, and the fatal gripe.
>
> (IV.i.14–19)

But once Francisco is alone he reveals in soliloquy that his reluctance was feigned and he has covert plans of his own which Monticelso will not even guess at: 'Thou canst not reach what I intend to act.' Monticelso provides him with a convenient list of villains for hiring, and, with this in hand, he summons up a mental image of the dead Isabella, represented onstage as the appearance of her ghost. He is now transformed into the revenger, eager for action, fertile of plots:

> Did ever
> Man dream awake till now – Remove this object,
> Out of my brain with't: what have I to do
> With tombs, or death-beds, funerals, or tears,
> That have to meditate upon revenge?
>   ... Come, to this weighty business.
>
> (IV.i.111–18)

The tone of this soliloquy is strange; it is as if Webster is making Francisco share the audience's awareness that he is a character in a revenge play who must act in a particular manner. The way in which the ghost is summoned up especially suggests this, with its almost comic promptness in appearing underlined by Francisco's comment, 'how strong/Imagination works'; this seems like a nudge to the audience, to take the speech as parody rather than a serious version of the revenger's vow. Francisco proceeds to outline his strategy:

> Come, to this weighty business.
> My tragedy must have some idle mirth in't,
> Else it will never pass. I am in love,
> In love with Corombona, and my suit
> Thus halts to her in verse –
> I have done it rarely

(IV.i.118–23)

The phrase 'this weighty business' again implies that the playwright is using the character's words to comment on the play itself, even reflecting on the seriousness of writing such a play at all. As J. R. Mulryne suggests in his article *'The White Devil* and *The Duchess of Malfi'*, 'This is the extreme point to which mockery can go.'

The mechanics of the revenge plot are speedily dealt with. Francisco decides that Lodovico will be his instrument, and, when the Count in his turn seems reluctant, having been vigorously dissuaded from violence by the suddenly-changed Monticelso, bribes him with a thousand crowns, ostensibly sent with Monticelso's blessing. In the last act a conventional revenge takes place. Francisco infiltrates Brachiano's court in disguise, a traditional device of the revenger to get the better of his enemies, and gathers round him a secret band of conspirators who consecrate themselves to the task, as symbolized in the embrace of Carlo, Gasparo and Pedro, all disguised, in V.i. The plot against Brachiano is to be an ingenious one, and although Francisco at one point hankers after something more public and ostentatious by way of revenge – 'To have tane him by the casque in a pitch'd field,/Led him to Florence' (V.i.81) – Lodovico is delighted by the manner in which Brachiano's death is brought about, especially the final strangling:

> No woman-keeper i'th' world,
> Though she had practis'd seven year at the pest-house,
> Could have done't quaintlier.

(V.iii.178–80)

Francisco has the pleasure, although he cannot acknowledge it because he is in disguise, of hearing Flamineo praise the skill of the murder – 'O the rare tricks of a Machivillian!'

A variation on this revenge action is performed in the final scene of the play. It says much for Webster's ingenuity that he still has means at his disposal to provide a more sensational death scene for Vittoria and Flamineo than even Brachiano's. Now it is Lodovico's turn to take the stage as revenger, and Francisco bows out, vowing to commemorate Lodovico's memory should he die in the action. But Webster is a master of the art of surprise, and for the first half of the scene it seems as if Vittoria and Flamineo may eliminate one another without outside help. Vittoria tricks her brother with a fake suicide pact, as he tricks her with fake bullets; when all the deceptions are revealed and the fictions of suicide and death enacted it is time for the truth; Lodovico and his disguised conspirators burst in through doors supposed locked with the ironic greeting: 'We have brought you a masque.' The revengers have only just enough time to complete the killings before there is another intrusion, this time by the forces of order: Prince Giovanni and the guards. Lodovico, wounded, is taken off to prison, but not before he has been allowed the revenger's last speech of triumphant self-assertion:

> I do glory yet
> That I can call this act mine own . . .
> *I limb'd this night-piece and it was my best.*

> (V.vi.291–5)

Power

Interwoven with the convolutions of the revenge plotting in *The White Devil* is the theme of the struggle for power. All of the characters pay allegiance to one or other of the two great Princes, Francisco and Brachiano, and the increasing polarization between the two factions is an important element in the shaping of the play. We should think of these Dukes less in terms of English noblemen, powerful within their own limited territory but ultimately members of a hierarchy owing fealty to a sole monarch, than of Italian Renaissance Princes, sole secular authorities within their own principalities, which could be of considerable size, and owing only religious allegiance to the Pope. These Princes usually sought to establish or perpetuate a dynastic claim, like the

Visconti-Sforza dynasty which ruled Milan and much of Lombardy for two hundred years, the Gonzaga dynasty in Mantua, the Este dynasty in Ferrara and of course the Medici in Florence, of which family Francisco and Isabella in the play are members. The Orsini, Brachiano's family, rose to prominence in Rome during the second half of the thirteenth century and later served under the Borgias. Although it is the adulterous love affair of Vittoria and Brachiano, and its repercussions, from which the plot of the play originates, the power politics of these two great families are far more than mere background material. Throughout the play Webster builds up a conception of the meaning of courtly power to those who wield it and those over whom it is exercised; he does this partly by means of direct illustrations through the behaviour of the princes and their underlings, and partly by the frequent use of generalized references in the dialogue, often in the form of sententious couplets, to great men and princes:

> Great men sell sheep, thus to be cut in pieces,
> When first they have shorn them bare and sold their fleeces.
>
> (I.i.61–2)

> Both flowers and weeds spring when the sun is warm,
> And great men do great good, or else great harm.
>
> (II.ii.56–7)

> He spreads his bounty with a sowing hand,
> Like kings, who many times give out of measure;
> Not for desert so much as for their pleasure.
>
> (IV.iii.85–7)

> Glories, like glow-worms, afar off shine bright
> But look'd to near, have neither heat nor light.
>
> (V.i.41–2)

> Court promises! Let wise men count them curs'd
> For while you live he that scores best pays worst.
>
> (V.iii.190–1)

> O happy they that never saw the court,
> *Nor ever knew great man but by report.*
>
> (V.vi.259–60)

References of this sort focus attention on the particular situation of great men, and the way in which their behaviour impinges directly on the lives of their dependents. The ideal relationship between Prince and people is defined in a truism given to Cornelia:

> The lives of princes should like dials move,
> Whose regular example is so strong,
> They make the times by them go right or wrong.
>
> (I.ii.285–7)

But these lines stand out in the play as an expression of an abstract moral norm which exists only as a distant possibility and bears no relation to any of these Princes. More relevant are the expressions of the vulnerability of Princes and their isolation. Their power is immense but it is autocratic and without any basis in social sanction; their dependents are bound not by ties of respect or of tradition, but by a bond of self-interest, which is quickly severed. This is the world of Machiavelli, where Princes must work all the time to maintain their positions and the smallest slip can bring a fall; and though they may not be virtuous in fact they must project the image of virtue, for without it they cannot succeed.

> Wretched are princes
> When fortune blasteth but a petty flower
> Of their unwieldy crowns; or ravisheth
> But one pearl from their sceptre: but alas!
> When they to wilful shipwreck lose good fame
> All princely titles perish with their name.
>
> (II.i.37–42)

A Prince needs to be feared rather than loved, and there are times when he will suffer on this account. During his last moments Brachiano is painfully aware of the difference between 'soft natural death' and his own: 'Pity winds thy corse,/Whilst horror waits on princes.' Flamineo, who owes him most, has no words of love or grief for his dying master; instead he stands back wryly to generalize from Brachiano's predicament:

To see what solitariness is about dying princes. As heretofore they have unpeopled towns; divorc'd friends, and made great houses unhospitable: so now, O justice! where are their flatterers now? Flatterers are but the shadows of princes' bodies, the least thick cloud makes them invisible.

> (V.iii.42–7)

The fluctuating fortunes of the man who, for whatever reason, makes or finds himself dependent on a Prince for the fulfilment of his own ambitions are traced in the careers of Lodovico and Flamineo. At the beginning of the play when Lodovico learns of his banishment he responds with bitter laughter:

> Ha, ha, O Democritus thy gods
> That govern the whole world! Courtly reward,
> And punishment!

(I.i.2–4)

The word 'courtly' carries a weight of irony. It refers not to the idea of the court as the wellspring of courtesy, as Spenser suggests in *The Faerie Queene* –

> Of court it seems, men Courtesie doe call,
> For that it there most useth to abound;
> And well beseemeth that in Princes hall
> That vertue should be plentifully found,
> Which of all goodly manners is the ground,
> And roote of ciuill conuersation

(VI.i.1–6)

– but to a court which represents the combination of arbitrary power and corruption. Flamineo twists the meaning of the word in the same way when describing his career in society:

> I visited the court, when I return'd
> More courteous, more lecherous by far,
> But not a suit the richer.

(I.ii.323–5)

Vittoria's couplet as she dies –

> O happy they that never saw the court,
> *Nor ever knew great man but by report*

(V.vi.259)

– expresses as a commonplace the idea that no profit is to be made by attending on Princes. For these characters court life is a rat-race, where success and failure are dependent entirely on the whims of those in power and bear no relation to desert. Lodovico, it seems from the expositionary comments of his friends Antonelli and Gasparo, has been 'justly doom'd' for many serious crimes; he is bitter not because he believes himself innocent – far from it – but for other reasons: in his society crime is a matter of course and his own murders are mere 'flea-bitings' to those committed by others who get off scot-free because they are of higher social rank. Furthermore, pardon may be granted, not for repentance or atonement, but merely on a personal whim; Vittoria could have saved Lodovico from his fate with 'one kiss to the Duke'. But the arbitrariness of the system, which causes Lodovico to be so resentful at his banishment, later works in his favour; Duke Francisco reports in II.i that Lodovico is engineering his return, but he expresses no anger at the

Count's belittling of his punishment, rather approval, and when Lodovico reappears in Rome Francisco soon procures him an official pardon with, presumably, retrospective force. Francisco has actually overridden the sanctions of law in order to ensure Lodovico's return and also, of course, to buy his loyalty; in order that the audience be fully aware of this Webster provides a scene in which Francisco is shown alone with his new dependent after the election of the Pope, and then has Monticelso question Lodovico about Francisco's actions:

> Why did the Duke of Florence with such care
> Labour your pardon? Say.
>
> (IV.iii.80–81)

Lodovico answers cynically, conscious of the self-interested nature of Francisco's action and without any sense of deference due to the newly elected Pope:

> Italian beggars will resolve you that
> Who, begging of an alms, bid those they beg of
> Do good for their own sakes.
>
> (IV.iii.82–4)

The partnership that Francisco forms with Lodovico, whom he has chosen to assist him in the revenge against Brachiano and Vittoria, becomes a close one, and Lodovico even begs his master to consider his own safety and take no part in the final killings. He takes upon him Francisco's cause and makes it his own, and although he is destined to die, tasting the justice of the new regime of Prince Giovanni, he considers himself well rewarded for the service he has undertaken:

> I do glory yet
> That I can call this act mine own.
>
> (V.vi.291–2)

Flamineo's career in the service of a Prince follows a completely different pattern, but it demonstrates even better than Lodovico's the chanciness of life as a court dependent. He has quite an important official position as the Duke's secretary, which would have meant acting as Brachiano's agent in all sorts of official business; he has attained it both by qualifications, in the form of seven years at university, and by ambition, and he is prepared to do anything at all to win his master's approval and so further his own progress. When Cornelia berates him for his lack of moral scruples in acting as pander for his own sister he justifies his behaviour in socio-economic terms; after a youth spent in genteel poverty he cannot neglect this fine opportunity for advancement:

> shall I,
> Having a path so open and so free
> To my preferment, still retain your milk
> In my pale forehead?

(I.ii.325–8)

He recognizes the existence of those standards of moral behaviour which would cause him 'shame and blushing' should he assess his own actions in their light, but he is prepared to set them aside. Great men such as Brachiano and Monticelso need not confine themselves within conventional moral limits, and Flamineo models his moral life on theirs. His brother Marcello is also a great man's dependent but by contrast offers only legitimate services, and, as Flamineo points out, has made no profit by them;

> Thou hast scarce maintenance
> To keep thee in fresh chamois.

(III.i.46–7)

The way of life Flamineo has chosen involves him in risks, but he feels that 'in our quest of gain' there is no alternative. He is prepared to endure uncertainty and even social humiliation in order to rise in the world, yet he is also resentful of his dependent and inferior position. On one occasion he allows this resentment against Brachiano to surface; and this impolitic outburst is remembered, and puts him yet more securely in his master's power. Brachiano, tricked by Francisco's letter to Vittoria into thinking her unfaithful, calls her a whore to her brother's face. Flamineo treats this as an insult and reacts violently; Brachiano is amazed and outraged at his servant's revolt:

BRACHIANO: In you pandar!
FLAMINEO: What me, my lord, am I your dog?
BRACHIANO: A blood-hound: do you brave? do you stand me?
FLAMINEO: Stand you? Let those that have diseases run.
           I need no plasters . . .
BRACHIANO: Do you know me?
FLAMINEO: O my lord! methodically.
           As in this world there are degrees of evils:
           So in this world there are degrees of devils.
           You're a great Duke; I your poor secretary.

(IV.ii.49–60)

When Flamineo finds himself most in need of his master's special favour, having murdered his brother, Brachiano uses the opportunity to display his power; he will keep the murder secret, but he will not pardon Flamineo, allowing him only a daily lease of life which must be begged for each evening:

> You once did brave me in your sister's lodging;
> I'll now keep you in awe for't.

When Brachiano dies, Flamineo shows no grief or remorse; his only thought is for the wasted service:

> Why here's an end of all my harvest, he has given me nothing,
> Court promises! Let wise me count them curs'd
> For while you live he that scores best pays worst.

> (V.iii.189–91)

The bond of self-interest between master and servant has served neither of them well: Flamineo, for all his scheming, cannot outwit Francisco, the real Machiavellian of the play, or save Brachiano, and Brachiano's death is the more terrible because he is a Prince. Without his master to protect him, Flamineo is thrown back on his own resources; if his death is less pitiful than Brachiano's, it is no less isolated.

The fortunes of all the characters, with the exception of Monticelso, are bound up with those of their masters, and the rapidly developed enmity between Francisco and Brachiano dominates the play. It is Brachiano's overwhelming passion for Vittoria which precipitates the feud. He promises grandly to seat her 'above law and above scandal'; he will devote his entire resources – 'dukedom, health, wife, children, friends and all' – to her pleasure. This single-minded intensity makes him rash and careless when Francisco, operating on behalf of his sister and of their family honour, warns him against pursuing his adulterous affair. Brachiano, full of guilty rage, vents his feelings about Francisco on Isabella, in a speech whose disjointed syntax and irrationally framed argument brilliantly express loss of self-control:

> Because your brother is the corpulent Duke,
> That is the great Duke, 'sdeath I shall not shortly
> Racket away five hundred crowns at tennis,
> But it shall rest upon record. I scorn him
> Like a shav'd Polack; all his reverent wit
> Lies in his wardrobe; he's a discreet fellow
> When he's made up in his robes of state –
> Your brother the great Duke, because h'as galleys,

> And now and then ransacks a Turkish fly-boat,
> (Now all the hellish Furies take his soul,)
> First made this match, – accursed be the priest
> That sang the wedding mass, and even my issue.

(II.i.180–91)

Brachiano tries to ridicule his adversary's power in jealous sniping at 'the corpulent Duke' with his 'robes of state' and his naval achievements. Francisco is his rival, and the unfortunate Isabella, like Octavia in *Antony and Cleopatra*, is only a pawn in the developing battle between her husband and her brother. Francisco seems initially the more controlled and disinterested of the two, chiefly desirous of Brachiano's reform and return to his duties as a Prince. At the end of II.i he associates himself with Monticelso's plan to shame Brachiano into self-awareness by arranging Camillo's absence so that the lovers may consummate their affair:

> I fain would have the Duke Brachiano run
> Into notorious scandal, for there's nought
> In such curs'd dotage, to repair his name,
> Only the deep sense of some deathless shame.

(II.i.385–8)

His warmth towards his nephew Giovanni earlier in this scene seems intended to show that at this time his motives are sincere; he urges Brachiano to set his son a good example. Consequently at this stage of the play the stress falls heavily on Brachiano's anti-social and irrational behaviour. Nonetheless it is Vittoria who is arrested and put on trial for complicity in her husband's murder; Brachiano is free to come and go as he likes. His very appearance in the court scene is an act of confrontation. Francisco does not expect him to come; this would be 'impudence too palpable' even for Brachiano. He behaves with a witty arrogance, outmanoeuvring the efforts of Monticelso and Francisco to embarrass him by providing his own place to sit in court, on a rich gown which, with a lordly gesture, he leaves behind as he departs – 'Brachiano/Was ne'er so beggarly, to take a stool/Out of another's lodging.' This air of casual impudence is belied by the threat in his parting words: 'Monticelso,/*Nemo me impune lacessit*' (III.ii.178). After the trial comes the public announcement of Isabella's death, but even so it is some time before open war between Brachiano and Francisco is declared. Francisco seems at first reluctant to take revenge for his sister's death, but a short soliloquy makes it clear that this is only a pose:

> Monticelso,
> I will not trust thee, but in all my plots
> I'll rest as jealous as a town besieg'd,
> Thou canst not reach what I intend to act.

> (IV.i.38–40)

The appearance, later in the same scene, of Isabella's ghost gives him the opportunity for an unambiguous declaration of intent but also subsumes the rivalry between the two Dukes into the more conventional pattern of a revenge plot, in which Francisco now takes on the role of scheming revenger whose tricks and stratagems are too skilful for his enemy to outwit. In the manipulation of his revenge plot in this part of the play Webster constantly keeps the audience one stage behind, so that the finale is managed by a series of surprises. Francisco's deceiving letter sent to Vittoria in the house of convertites seems at first to have achieved the opposite of what he intended, in that it brings about a reconciliation between the lovers rather than a split. But when Francisco hears that they have run away together, he is triumphant:

> How fortunate are my wishes. Why? 'Twas this
> I only labour'd. I did send the letter
> T'instruct him what to do.

> (IV.iii.52–4)

When the audience learns, from Flamineo's information, that Brachiano has acquired the support of an eminent, Othello-like Moorish nobleman, newly arrived at court to help in wars against Francisco, it seems once more as if Brachiano is in the ascendant, but of course the Moor turns out to be Francisco in disguise, and this particular stratagem, which fools Brachiano and all his court, is Francisco's trump card. It allows for some moments of dramatic irony at the expense of both Brachiano and of Flamineo. The former, realizing he has been poisoned, guesses rightly at the source: 'This unction is sent from the great Duke of Florence.' What he does not realize of course is that the poisoner is actually standing at his side, appearing to offer comfort. Similarly, after Brachiano's death Francisco is confident enough of his disguise to suggest to Flamineo where the responsibility lies: 'Sure, this was Florence' doing.' Flamineo agrees:

> Very likely.
> Those are found weighty strokes which came from th'hand,
> But those are killing strokes which come from th'head.
> O the rare tricks of a Machivillian!

> (V.iii.192–5)

Francisco fools his enemies to the last, and the final triumph is his *in absentia*. Vittoria, submitting to the inevitability of death, wishes she might meet it at Francisco's hands, but Gasparo points out how naïve this is:

> Fool! Princes give rewards with their own hands,
> But death or punishment by the hands of others.

> (V.vi.186–7)

It is part of Francisco's victory that he has no longer any need to be present or involved. His power is the greater for being administered through agents. The Prince is above and outside the patterns which shape the lives of ordinary mortals. When Giovanni and his guards break in on the scene of slaughter, Francisco is not there to be taken to justice. And from what the play has shown of power and privilege it seems safe to assume that the forces of law and order which conventionally assert themselves at the conclusion of a revenge tragedy can exercise no sanctions over him.

Integrity of Life

The play has much to show of power and ambition, and of the strategies necessary to succeed in court life. The main characters, Brachiano, Vittoria, Francisco and Flamineo, are strong, ruthless individuals who are displayed acting for their own interests without any consideration for the welfare of a wider community. The weaker characters, Isabella, Camillo, Marcello and Cornelia, are progressively destroyed. Webster's depiction of this dangerous and insecure world is not detached or objective. He does not construct his characters and situations so as to leave us unmoved, with only an intellectual response, as Brecht might. The action is often violent and horrific, but it is also exciting and in-volving, partly because of the strong passions which motivate the characters, and of the dramatic conviction in their portrayal. This is indeed a deeply felt vision of life, but is it a tragic one? That we are moved by the fates of these characters, at least by some of them, is an indication that it is. But with a play so rich in dramatic effects as this it is necessary to distinguish between local effects of horror, pathos, excitement and other forms of audience arousal typical of Jacobean drama, and larger impressions formed in response to the play as a whole. What feelings are we left with at the end of a reading or a performance of *The White Devil*? What meanings can be discovered in the events and action of the play? There are certain kinds of consolations provided at the end of a tragedy which are clearly not on offer here, no 'flights of angels' to sing the dying characters to their rest, for instance, no tributes to their greatness by the survivors. In general this is a play which avoids conventional solutions; the most significant mouthpiece of traditional morality, Cornelia, who expresses accepted attitudes towards duty, family life and the responsibilities of Princes, is both literally and figuratively a background figure, whose words make no impact at all on the behaviour of the other characters, and whose ultimate lapse into madness seems to signify her ineffectuality. As has been mentioned already, a majority of the sententious couplets, which are so prominent a feature of the play's dramatic language, do not express conventional moral sentiments at all, or if they do, not in such a way that the play endorses them. Monticelso's exemplary advice to Brachiano to reform his behaviour so as to leave a permanent image of virtue for his son to imitate –

> Leave him a stock of virtue that may last,
> Should fortune rend his sails, and split his mast
>
> (II.i.106–107)

– is not a disinterested and objective piece of moralizing, since Monticelso has a personal stake in achieving Brachiano's reform. When Francisco has heard that the first stage of his revenge against Brachiano has been successful, he prepares for the next events with the words –

> The hand must act to drown the passionate tongue,
> I scorn to wear a sword and prate of wrong.
>
> (IV.iii.57–8)

The sentiment (adapted by Webster from some very similar lines in *Julius Caesar*, a play of 1607 by Sir William Alexander) is not, as it might seem, out of context, a solemn commitment to positive moral action instead of mere verbal declaration, but rather a declaration in favour of violence. In the play's first scene Lodovico's companions Gasparo and Antonelli attempt to reconcile him to the prospect of banishment with a series of impeccably moral generalizations, some of them in jarringly trite couplets:

> O my lord
> The law doth sometimes mediate, thinks it good
> Not ever to steep violent sins in blood;
> This gentle penance may both end your crimes,
> And in the example better those bad times.
>
> (I.i.33–7)

But Lodovico cuts short their flow with dismissive bitterness:

> Leave your painted comforts.
> I'll make Italian cut-works in their guts
> If ever I return.

(I.i.50–2)

'Painted comforts', the consoling view of human life as governed by a moral power and ultimately susceptible to rational interpretation, is rejected in *The White Devil*. It is not always easy to discern truth in this play of deceptive appearances, but Webster does sometimes discriminate between truth and appearance by various means, for instance allowing his characters scenes of deliberate role-playing, which can be explicitly compared with scenes of uncalculated behaviour, or by the use of asides and comments addressed to the audience, and even, occasionally, explanatory soliloquies. In I.ii, for example, Flamineo quite clearly plays one part for Camillo, pretending as his brother-in-law to give him helpful advice on his marital relations, and another part for Vittoria, in collusion against Camillo; a soliloquy at the end of the scene, though not personally revelatory, provides a few moments for the character to drop his mask and speak in his own voice. In II.i Isabella also enacts a role intended to deceive onlookers when she pretends, in front of Francisco and Monticelso, that it is she, not Brachiano, who is eager for a separation between them. She devises and performs a little playlet, and the contrivance is clearly signalled in an expository speech which totally takes in its audience (though not, of course, the audience in the theatre), where she asks her husband's assistance in hiding the truth from her brother:

> Conceal it I beseech you, for the weal
> Of both your dukedoms, that you wrought the means
> Of such a separation; let the fault
> Remain with my supposed jealousy,
> And think with what a piteous and rent heart
> I shall perform this sad ensuing part.

(II.i.219–24)

In the play's final scene, Flamineo's contrivance with the unloaded pistols and Vittoria's and Zanche's fake suicide pact allow the characters grand opportunities for playing out false death scenes before they die in earnest. When Flamineo presents Vittoria and Zanche with two cases of pistols instead of the 'two case of jewels' which he says Brachiano has bequeathed him, the women recoil in horror, recognizing that he means to kill them. Vittoria initially tries to dissuade her brother but, failing, colludes in a plan with Zanche, which they devise in hasty asides, to form a suicide pact with Flamineo, get him to die first, and then renege on their promise. Vittoria's grand 'dying' speech addressed to Brachiano at V.vi.81 ('Behold Brachiano, I that while you liv'd . . .') is clearly perceived by the audience as play-acting for Flamineo's benefit, although the tone seems to convey a convincing ardour. Zanche, too, opts for a noble style of death:

> How madam! Do you think that I'll outlive you?
> Especially when my best self Flamineo
> Goes the same voyage.
>
> (V.vi.85–7)

On stage, these splendid sentiments might be delivered in such a way as to capitalize on the audience's awareness that they are not genuine, but although, as it turns out, Flamineo's 'dying' speech is also a fake, neither his onstage audience nor the audience in the theatre know it at the time. Where Vittoria and Zanche choose to present themselves dying nobly and selflessly, Flamineo adopts an attitude of characteristic scepticism:

> Whether I resolve to fire, earth, water, air,
> Or all the elements by scruples, I know not
> Nor greatly care.
>
> (V.vi.111–13)

When the time comes for the characters to die in earnest the postures enacted earlier are substantially repeated. But the distinction between their play-acting selves and their real selves seems to be that whereas they all adopted stratagems to avoid dying in the first part of the scene, pretending the while to act courageously, now that death is inevitable all three of them accept it stoically. Vittoria and Zanche insist on their own fearlessness, and Vittoria taunts her murderers with their lack of valour:

> 'Twas a manly blow.
> The next thou giv'st, murder some sucking infant,
> And then thou wilt be famous.
>
> (V.vi.230–2)

Her bravery is admired by Gasparo and by Flamineo, who speaks as if proud to claim kinship with her:

> Th'art a noble sister,
> I love thee now; if woman do breed man
> She ought to teach him manhood. Fare thee well.
>
> (V.vi.39–41)

In dying neither Vittoria and Flamineo expects any consolation in the afterlife, so that their courage at the last moment of their lives is disinterested. Flamineo is only glad that death will end life's uncertainty: *'We cease to grieve, cease to be Fortune's slaves,/Nay cease to die by dying.'* It is this courage, so late to be revealed in the play, but so definitive, coming as it does after the false death scenes, that resounds at the conclusion and gives conviction to the claims made by several of the characters to some kind of transcendent quality, for which perhaps *'virtu'* in the Italian sense of magnificent boldness or decisiveness is more appropriate than 'virtue'. Several expressions of praise and admiration using such terms as 'noble' or 'glorious' are to be found in the latter half of the play, and these, even if they do not always command an audience's full endorsement, at least help to direct our responses. The revenge masterminded by Francisco is to be not a utilitarian but a glorious deed; this evaluation has something of the aesthetic in it, in that the conspirators, Lodovico particularly, are eager for an 'ingenious' or 'quaint' plot, and when the execution of murders is complete Lodovico refers to the deed as a masterpiece of art: *'I limb'd this night-piece and it was my best'* (V.vi.295). Skill in contrivance is a quality to be admired, but so too is courage, and just as the confrontation with death calls forth the courage of the victim, so too are the revengers ready to meet their own fate without flinching when it comes upon them. Flamineo in his last speech bids, 'Farewell glorious villains,' referring presumably both to the revengers as well as Vittoria and Zanche. He has earlier classed Vittoria with those 'glorious women . . . fam'd/For masculine virtue' whose moral viciousness does not detract from their quality. Ultimately, the elements of corruption in the major characters are not denied or glossed over, but Webster allows them to co-exist with a kind of defiance and self-assertiveness which makes these characters shine gloriously in the dark and chaotic world they inhabit.

7. Stagecraft

Although *The White Devil* makes use of many of the accepted stage devices of the Italianate revenge play, some of them probably rather old-fashioned by this time, it is nonetheless exciting and original as a piece of stagecraft. Webster has chosen to represent a sequence of events stemming from a single initial act of passion, but he does this, not by dramatizing a fluid series, but rather by depicting only selected high points in the sequence that takes place between the time when the illicit love of Brachiano and Vittoria is consummated and the ultimate deaths of all involved. Those events Webster chooses to represent onstage are not necessarily inherently more dramatic than those which are recounted in narration, such as Vittoria's escape from the house of convertites, or depicted only symbolically, like the deaths of Camillo and Isabella; but by telescoping his action in this way Webster gives pace and variation to his play and intensifies his focus on certain special moments in his characters' lives, Isabella's final scene with her husband, for instance, or Vittoria's trial.

Webster's use of the devices of revenge drama is never merely slavish or imitative; they contribute importantly to the craft of the play as well as helping to underline one of its themes: that life is a spectacle in which one has often to play a part for the benefit of others. The first such device occurs in II.ii in the use of dumbshow to depict the murders of Isabella and Camillo. This archaic technique, derived from the religious and civic shows of the late Middle Ages and their tradition of incorporating meaning in visual emblems, could be used as a means of giving an allegorical or simplified summary of events which were subsequently acted out, as in *Hamlet*, for instance, but here Webster speeds things up by dispensing with the full-scale enactment, and telescoping the two murders into a single scene where Brachiano is given a vision of the future by a conjurer. Thus the deaths of Isabella and Camillo are rendered less immediate to the audience, and attention is focused instead on Brachiano and the nature of his responses. The passing of time is greatly speeded up, for the next scene shows Francisco and Monticelso preparing for Vittoria's trial. The 'antic disposition' which Flamineo adopts after the trial in order to evade questioning about the murder of Isabella is another convention of revenge drama; Hieronimo in *The Spanish Tragedy* and Hamlet feign madness in order to divert their enemies from probing their behaviour too closely, and Vindice, in *The Revenger's Tragedy*, adopts, like Hamlet, the role of cynic and malcontent in order to further his revenge; Flamineo here signals his intention clearly:

Because now I cannot counterfeit a whining passion for the death of my lady, I will feign a mad humour for the disgrace of my sister, and that will keep off idle questions.

(III.ii.303–306)

The humour enables him to express cynical truths to the foreign ambassadors but it does not deceive Lodovico, who, being a plotter himself, recognizes Flamineo's game. It serves him well with Brachiano, however, and he draws the audience's attention to the usefulness of his mad act in an aside at the end of IV.ii:

> It may appear to some ridiculous
> Thus to talk knave and madman . . .
> But this allows my varying of shapes,
> *Knaves do grow great by being great men's apes.*

(IV.ii.241–5)

The pointing of a contrast between this kind of feigned distraction, which gives a freedom to make satirical jibes and bitter witticisms, and the real madness of another character in the play is also a common feature of revenge tragedy. Here Flamineo's discursive and malcontented style is sharply distinguished from the idiom given to Cornelia in her madness; she combines the pathetic quality of Ophelia with her distribution of herbs to her audience and her sad dirge for Marcello with the more ominous notes borrowed from the sleepwalking of Lady Macbeth. Her speech has a kind of stilted innocence in its childish rhymes:

> Can blood so soon be wash'd out? Let me see:
> When screech-owls croak upon the chimney tops,
> And the strange cricket i'th' oven sings and hops,
> When yellow spots do on your hands appear,
> Be certain then you of a corse shall hear.
> Out upon't, how 'tis speckled! H'as handled a toad sure.

(V.iv.82–7)

In addition to this relatively conventional contrasting of styles of distraction Webster gives us also Brachiano's brain-softening, as he succumbs gradually to the effects of poison. His ramblings, like those of many mad characters, mix sense and nonsense, but also make explicit such preoccupations as he may be presumed to have had, though without expressing them, when he was sane. He talks of his duties as a ruler – 'battles and monopolies, / levying of taxes' – and descends to 'most brain-sick language' in hallucinations about the devil in a codpiece in his bedroom and grey rats crawling up his pillow. Where Cornelia's form of madness is feminine and pathetic, Brachiano's is savage and horrifying; the daring stroke of depicting the two in successive scenes of the play's last act contributes to the variety of sensational effect so remarkable in the dénouement.

Disguise is another conventional device of revenge tragedy which Webster generally integrates very fully into the plot of *The White Devil*. Flamineo's feigned distraction is in itself a kind of disguise, of feelings if not of appearance, though this is important for his role of malcontent rather than for the plot. The disguise of the conspirators in the last act as Capuchin monks, though not original, creates a wittily ironic effect when they pretend to administer the last rites to Brachiano. But it is the disguise of Francisco as Mulinassar the Moor on which the successful achievement of the revenge depends. The audience is not immediately let into the secret of his disguise, so that we are the more prepared for the characters in the play to be totally fooled by it. When Flamineo and Hortensio at the beginning of Act V admiringly discuss 'the Moor that's come to court', his warlike manner and his experience in courtly ways, there is no clue to the audience as to this Moor's true identity, and it may not be evident when he makes his appearance with Brachiano, at V.i.43, welcomed as an honoured guest to the marriage festivities. Perhaps the moment of revelation for the audience is delayed until line 63, when Brachiano and his followers leave the stage, and the con-spirators, including the disguised Francisco, formally embrace. That Flamineo is utterly duped by Francisco's plot is carefully brought out in an exchange between them after Brachiano's death, when Flamineo comments bitterly on his unrewarded service; referring to the manner of Brachiano's death Francisco asserts daringly, 'Sure, this was Florence' doing', and Flamineo responds innocently with bitter praise for the cunning contrivance of the death: 'O the rare tricks of a Machivillian' (V.iii.195). Vittoria's deception too is signalled to the audience, in her wish that, 'If Florence be i'th' court, would he would kill me.' Francisco's disguise takes in everyone, and even Giovanni who enters with the guards to restore order at the end of the play is amazed to learn of his uncle's trick. The disguise illuminates Francisco's role as the arch-plotter in a world where almost everyone seems to be engaged in some kind of deception, and diminishes Flamineo's success as a manipulator; he emerges as the deceiver deceived, the 'engineer hoist with his own petard'.

Francisco's disguise, though a conventional device, is brilliantly used, both to bring about the play's dénouement and to demonstrate the meaning of courtly power. Francisco emerges at his most triumphant *in absentia*; the very fact that he is not present at the ritual round-up of the murderers in the final scene signifies his successful evasion of justice and also casts a dark shadow over the hopeful moralizing of the new young ruler. The two ghosts, of Isabella and later of Brachiano, an equally conventional element in revenge drama, are, however, much less well integrated into the play. There seems to be a kind of hesitancy, or, more likely, scepticism, about the way in which Isabella's ghost is made to appear when Francisco summons up the image of his dead sister in order to harden his resolve for revenge; he himself is uncertain as to the nature of the apparition:

> Thought, as a subtle juggler, makes us deem
> Things supernatural, which have cause
> Common as sickness. 'Tis my melancholy.

(IV.i.107–109)

And when he commands, 'Remove this object,' the ghost duly departs and is never seen or mentioned again. It is given no necessary function in the play, and Francisco's soliloquy vowing revenge could easily have been constructed without it. Brachiano's ghost appears to Flamineo in V.iv and it is used to foretell the future, in that its action of throwing earth upon Flamineo and showing him a skull is correctly interpreted by him as an omen of death. In view of the fact that the ghost is produced so late on, in the last act of the play, its message is completely predictable, even redundant; nor is it made the instrument of any revelation about the character either of Flamineo or of Brachiano. Both ghosts appear largely because revenge tradition requires it, and Webster, rather than disguising this fact, almost appears to draw attention to it.

Two conventions of speech, the aside and the sententious couplet, are, however, used with considerable skill by Webster to quite other than conventional effect. The ironic use of the couplet has been referred to earlier (see p. 47). The conspicuously artificial quality of it, marked off as it is from ordinary dramatic speech by the rhyme, and expressive of sentiments in some way beyond the experience or else outside the character of the speaker, contributes towards an effect of distancing which is one of the most marked aspects of Webster's stagecraft, and produced by a combination of several means. The aside is one of these means, again a familiar convention of the Elizabethan and Jacobean stage, an inheritance from medieval drama, but in Webster's plays often put to a more imaginative use. Sometimes of course he employs the aside in the normal way, to convey information to the audience which is not intended for the ears of others present.

Thus Flamineo frequently explains his behaviour, when he is putting on an act for a specific purpose:

> I do put on this feigned garb of mirth
> To gull suspicion.

(III.i.2–3)

Because now I cannot counterfeit a whining passion for the death of my lady, I will feign a mad humour for the disgrace of my sister.

(III.ii.303–306)

> It may appear to some ridiculous
> Thus to talk knave and madman; . . .
> But this allows my varying of shapes.
>
> (IV.ii.241–4)

Other characters also use asides to provide information to the audience, for instance Francisco (IV.iii.52 and V.ii.81) or Zanche (V.i.214), but Flamineo is the most frequent and conspicuous speaker of them. Another less conventional use of the aside occurs in I.ii, when Cornelia makes an entry at line 204 unseen by the other characters, and remains upstage for about fifty lines listening and commenting in an aside to the audience before she enters the action proper, to predict doom for her family. Webster is here perhaps adapting a technique from Shakespeare's *Richard III* where old Queen Margaret makes her first entrance in the same way, and surprises the others present by her sudden doom-laden appearance. In both cases the unseen listener has a different perspective on the scene from the other characters, and her words to the audience come as those of one who has deeper insight into events than the other characters then onstage. Cornelia's presence in I.ii has, however, an extra dimension from Margaret's, in that the main action, that is, the intimate dialogue between the lovers Vittoria and Brachiano, is also observed from another angle, by Flamineo and Zanche who in their turn comment on the scene, unheard by the participants. What the audience sees, then, is three layers of action: the courtship of Vittoria and Brachiano, which is carried on without reference to anyone else onstage, the commentary of Zanche and especially Flamineo, whose cynical view of the lovers effectively debunks the romantic style and language of their encounter, and the commanding perspective of Cornelia, who sees both the lovers and her son's part in arranging their liaison, and counters Flamineo's amoral pleasure in the success of his pandering with her rigid disapproval.

This multi-layered use of the aside helps to create an important effect of detachment, in that the audience is invited to respond, not only to the encounter of the lovers, but also to the diverse responses made to it by the onstage observers. Thus what seems to be the central action is in fact presented to us at two removes. Webster relishes these complex perspectives, and provides for them in other ways, one of which derives from another use of the aside. Earlier in I.ii Flamineo is the central figure in a triangular action between himself, Vittoria and her husband Camillo. Here his asides are addressed to one or other of them, and he stage-manages the action so that husband and wife do not speak directly to one another until he has prepared a scene for them to play. At the entry of Camillo (I.ii.47) Flamineo in an aside to the audience expresses his real opinion of his brother-in-law as 'merely an ass in's foot-cloth', although in front of Camillo he pretends to be respectful and helpful in devising a method to repair the failing marriage. When Vittoria appears Flamineo adroitly manages by means of asides to his sister to appear to be speaking up for Camillo's rights as her husband, while at the same time insulting his brother-in-law grossly and arranging the circumstances for Vittoria to meet Brachiano. The effect of Flamineo's gulling of Camillo, who is quite convinced that his brother-in-law is acting in his best interests, when the reverse is, of course, the case, is extremely comic:

FLAMINEO: See she comes ... walk you aloof, I would not have you seen in't. Sister (my lord attends you in the banqueting-house), your husband is wondrous discontented.

VITTORIA: I did nothing to displease him, I carved to him at supper-time.

FLAMINEO: (You need not have carved him in faith, they say he is a capon already. I must now seemingly fall out with you.) Shall a gentleman so well descended as Camillo (a lousy slave that within this twenty years rode with the black-guard in the Duke's carriage 'mongst spits and dripping-pans.)

CAMILLO: Now he begins to tickle her.

(I.ii.114–33)

Having assured Camillo that his best ploy to regain Vittoria's affections will be to play at being cold and refuse to sleep with her, and having assured Vittoria that she will now have the opportunity to consummate her affair with Brachiano, Flamineo finally allows the couple to speak to one another and act out the scene he has arranged. Once Camillo has played his part and left the stage, Brachiano enters on cue, and the second scene of Flamineo's devising, the lovers' meeting, then takes place.

Flamineo's asides often put him in the position of a detached commentator, but the effect of this is never to imply that he is to be seen as the audience's viewpoint. His own attitudes are too clearly biased and corrupt for this to be the case. In IV.ii he again acts as a kind of intermediary, this time in the quarrel between Brachiano and Vittoria. Asides are again the medium by which he gives private advice to Brachiano on how to win Vittoria back after the quarrel while seeming to take Vittoria's part as wronged victim; he is also given a different kind of aside, addressed to the audience, which makes clear his true attitude of cynical debunking of the whole affair:

What a damn'd imposthume is a woman's will?
Can nothing break it? (*to* BRACHIANO, *aside*) Fie, fie, my lord.

Women are caught as you take tortoises,
She must be turn'd on her back. (*aloud*) Sister, by this hand
I am on your side. – Come, come, you have wrong'd her.
What a strange credulous man were you, my lord,
To think the Duke of Florence would love her?
(*aside*) Will any mercer take another's ware
When once 'tis tows'd and sullied? (*aloud*) And yet, sister,
How scurvily this frowardness becomes you!

(IV.ii.148–58)

Once again Flamineo appears as the manipulator; he needs, for his own advancement, to ensure that the breach between his sister and her powerful lover is healed, and his emotional detachment, combined with greater quickness of wit than the other participants in the action, puts him in a position of advantage for bringing about the reconciliation. But in the last scene of the play he is, at least momentarily, outwitted, and once again Webster devises a triangular encounter where two of the characters collude, by means of asides, against the third. Here the partners are Vittoria and Zanche, and it is Flamineo's turn to be victim. Vittoria, confronted unexpectedly by Flamineo's threat to murder her and kill himself temporizes by putting the religious argument against suicide, while attempting desperately in asides to arrange with Zanche for their rescue. Zanche comes up with a plan which she communicates privately to Vittoria:

ZANCHE (*aside*):   Gentle madam
        Seem to consent, only persuade him teach
        The way to death; let him die first.
VITTORIA (*aside*): 'Tis good, I apprehend it.
        (*aloud*): To kill oneself is meat that we must take
        Like pills, not chew't, but quickly swallow it.

(V.vi.70–5)

The women's trick seems initially to be working, until the apparently dying Flamineo rises unhurt, to reveal that the pistols were loaded with blanks. Here, the aside device recoils on the users; Vittoria and Zanche believe themselves to be deceivers but are in fact the deceived. Once again Flamineo's superior wit brings him out on top, though of course, as has been said, the outcome of the scene shows him outplayed by the arch-manipulator, Francisco.

Webster's stagecraft in *The White Devil* depends heavily on a variety of non-naturalistic devices; the audience is kept constantly aware of the fact that it is watching a theatrical representation, and one that itself depicts the lives of the participants as a theatrical spectacle. 'All the world's a stage' was a familiar maxim to the Jacobeans, and the consciousness that 'one man in his time plays many parts' is an explicit aspect of the characterization of Flamineo. Role-playing is inherent too in the make-up of Vittoria and of Francisco. It is not surprising then to find that the play makes much use of ceremony and ritual, forms of action in which the participants act out pre-designated parts, using formal speeches devised for them by others, and sometimes wearing special symbolic costumes. The Papal election in Act IV is the most obvious example of this, and it is thought that Webster followed his source, *A Treatise of the Election of Popes* by Hierome Bignon, quite closely in order to achieve an effect of authenticity. The trial of Vittoria is also a formal ceremony, conducted in the presence of foreign ambassadors, and, at least initially, with judicial procedures in Latin. The duelling display, or 'barriers', which Brachiano plans to celebrate his marriage to Vittoria, is another ritual, modelled on ceremonies which took place at the courts of Elizabeth I and James I on festive occasions, and no doubt intended to provide an opportunity for a spectacular display of swordsmanship by the actors, as the stage directions to V.iii (*'Charges and shouts. They fight at barriers; first single pairs, then three to three.'*) would suggest. The last act of the play is particularly well provided with ritual elements: the opening procession after the marriage, the barriers themselves, the mock administration of last rites to the dying Brachiano by Lodovico and Gasparo in the guise of Capuchins, the song sung over the winding of Marcello's corpse (V.iv.65), the appearance of Brachiano's ghost with its strange symbolic actions and, finally, the entry of masked revengers who break in on Flamineo, Vittoria and Zanche.

It has been noticed that the play is also marked by the use of inverted or parodied ritual, which adds to its overall quality of darkness and nightmarish horror. In the scene where Brachiano and Isabella part forever his rejection of her takes the form of a cancellation of the marriage ceremony in which the meaning of the usual ritual is entirely reversed. First he curses Isabella's brother, Francisco, as the maker of the match, and then the priest who celebrated it, and even his own issue. Then, ceremonially, he casts off Isabella as his wife:

> Your hand I'll kiss:
> This is the latest ceremony of my love,
> Henceforth I'll never lie with thee, by this,
> This wedding ring: I'll ne'er more lie with thee.
> And this divorce shall be as truly kept,
> As if the judge had doom'd it.

(II.i.192–7)

Blessings turn to curses, and the wedding ring is used to symbolize not union but divorce. Isabella echoes Brachiano's vow later in the scene when she pretends, in front of her brother, to be the active partner in the rift with her husband:

> Sir let me borrow of you but one kiss,
> Henceforth I'll never lie with you, by this,
> This wedding-ring . . .
> And this divorce shall be as truly kept,
> As if in thronged court, a thousand ears
> Had heard it.
>
> (II.i.252–7)

In III.ii Vittoria's trial rapidly turns into a parody, or, as she calls it, a 'rape' of justice, where Monticelso assumes the role of accuser as well as that of judge, and the conclusion is foregone. In IV.iii Lodovico's revelation of the revenge plot to Monticelso takes the form of a confession; Monticelso in his new role as Pope sternly warns Lodovico against the act, but his advice is instantly subverted by Francisco, who sees that a large bribe is supplied to Lodovico to pursue the revenge, ostensibly on Monticelso's secret orders. The most notable effect of inverted ritual occurs in the scene of Brachiano's death, where after the revengers in their disguise as Capuchin monks have spoken the last rites in Latin, they revert, when left alone, to English and reveal their true identities to the audience as well as to their victim when they torment him in his last moment with a hissed litany of hate:

> GASPARO: Brachiano
> LODOVICO: Devil Brachiano. Thou art damn'd.
> GASPARO: Perpetually.
> LODOVICO: A slave condemn'd, and given up to the gallows
>   Is thy great lord and master . . .
> GASPARO: This is Count Lodovico.
> LODOVICO: This Gasparo.
>   And thou shalt die like a poor rogue.
> GASPARO: And stink
>   Like a dead fly-blown dog.
> LODOVICO: And be forgotten before thy funeral sermon.
>
> (V.iii.151–4, 166–9)

There is a truly black comedy in the manner of Brachiano's death. Vittoria and her attendants, who have earlier been dismissed from the scene, return at an inappropriate moment, when Gasparo has given an order to finish off Brachiano by strangling, and have to be hurriedly sent away again:

GASPARO (*aside*): Strangle him in private.
        (*aloud*): What? Will you call him again
             To live in treble torments? For charity,
             For Christian charity, avoid the chamber.

                        (V.iii.172–5)

Brachiano is promptly dispatched, Lodovico congratulates himself on the skilful manner of the strangling, and within six lines Vittoria and company are back again to express conventional pieties over the corpse. 'Rest to his soul', though a line apparently suited to the occasion, sounds ludicrous here, the grotesque killing only just complete and the murderers standing by, privately overjoyed by their success.

By such means as these Webster creates a revenge tragedy which keeps the audience in a continuous state of excitement and surprise. Emotional effects are complex and unpredictable; for a tragedy there are many comic moments, but often laughter terminates abruptly in horror. The stagecraft is perfectly adapted to his vision of a world where many of the usual elements are present but displaced, or inverted, and the appearance of order and regularity is always a deception.

The Duchess of Malfi

1. Sources

The Duchess of Malfi is based on historical fact, but the story is obscure in comparison with that of *The White Devil*, and there is no doubt that Webster's main source for his play was not an Italian manuscript or other kind of factual account but William Painter's *Palace of Pleasure* (1567). This was a collection of moral tales, mostly tragic in nature, which Painter had translated from the French of Belleforest's *Histoiries Tragiques*, which in its time was a translation from the Italian of Bandello in his *Novelle* (1554). It seems that Bandello, the veracity of whose account is borne out by various manuscripts and other sources, actually knew Antonio and represented himself in the story as Delio, Antonio's friend and confidant who survives, like Horatio in *Hamlet*, to see the truth is told to the world. In real life the Duchess and her brothers were the grandchildren of Ferdinand I of Naples. The eldest, Ludovico, Webster's Cardinal, was precociously famous for swordsmanship, and had a brief but brilliant worldly career before renouncing his title in favour of his brother Carlo (Ferdinand) and becoming Cardinal of Aragon in 1494. Giovanna, their sister (the Duchess), married at twelve to the son of the Duke of Malfi, had two children of whom only a son survived, and was widowed eight years later, in 1498. She was very young, nineteen or twenty, when she met Antonio Bologna who had been in France with Federico of Naples, exiled after his kingdom had been partitioned; Antonio become steward to her household. They fell in love, were married in secret, and concealed their relationship for some years. After the birth of their second child the Duchess's brother began to grow suspicious and set spies on the couple. Antonio left for Ancona, taking the two children, and shortly afterwards the Duchess joined him, feigning a pilgrimage to Loretto. Her intention was to renounce her rank and live as a private person, but when her brothers got wind of this they pursued and hounded her and Antonio from place to place, and eventually the couple were forced to separate, Antonio and the eldest son departing for Milan, the Duchess and her younger children, two by now, retreating to one of her castles, from which it seems they never escaped alive. Antonio, ignorant of his wife's fate, hung on in Milan, surviving under the protection of a series of noblemen and hoping eventually to appease his brothers-in-law. But this never happened and he was murdered by a hired assassin, Daniel de Bosola, a Lombard captain, who made his escape with three others. One of the last people to see him alive was Delio, or rather Bandello himself, who saw Antonio on his way to Mass only moments before the assassination.

This bare narrative was much augmented by Belleforest, who changed or added certain details, such as that it was the waiting maid who suggested the pilgrimage to Loretto (in Webster it is Bosola), and that the Duchess met her death by strangulation. More important, perhaps, is the fact that Belleforest adopted a strongly moralistic attitude to the marriage which Painter reproduces in his translation; for instance the young Duchess in her widowhood is said to feel 'a certain unacquainted lust' and to be 'pressed with desire of match, to remove the ticklish instigations of hir wanton flesh'. Painter is especially indignant in his denunciation of the Duchess for agreeing to make the feigned pilgrimage to Loretto in order to be reunited with Antonio:

It was not sufficient for this foolish woman to take a husband, more to glut hir libidinous appetite, than for other occasion, except she added to hir sinne, an other execrable impietie, making holy places and dueties of deuotion, to be as it were the ministers of hir follie . . . who wold think that a great Ladie wold have abandoned hir estate, hir goods and childe, would have misprised hir honor and reputation, to follow like a vagabond, a pore and simple Gentleman, and him bisides that was the houshold seruaunt of hir Court?

(quoted from *The Duchess of Malfi*, ed. J. R. Brown, Revels edition, p. 195)

In assessing the distribution of sympathy in Webster's treatment of the marriage it is important to be aware of the kind of moral light in which he encountered the story. And it is also of significance that the Duchess's marriage was referred to in a number of other contemporary writings, such as Robert Greene's *Gwydonius: the Carde of Fancie* (1584), George Whetstone's *Heptameron of Civil Discourses* (1582) and Thomas Beard's *Theatre of Gods Judgments* (1597), amongst others, as an example of an unwise marriage between unequal partners, doomed to disaster. No doubt many of the audience for the play, even if unaware of the historical status of the characters, would have come with a preconceived attitude towards the situation.

Though the story of the play is substantially taken from Painter's translation of Belleforest there are, naturally, several significant changes and additions, some of which Webster found ideas for in other sources and some of which he invented. In the first part of the play Webster makes several circumstantial changes to the structure of events in the interests of intensifying the dramatic effect: the warnings of the Cardinal and Ferdinand against remarriage which are given immediately before the scene in which the Duchess woos Antonio are new, so too the manner of the discovery of the Duchess's guilt, by Antonio's dropping of the horoscope, which happens after the birth of the first child, not, as in Painter, after the second. The little scene of play-acting, in which the Duchess pretends to accuse Antonio of fraudulent dealing in order to contrive an excuse for his departure (III.ii.161–227), is also an addition. In the latter part of the play the suffering and tortures of the Duchess, for which Webster drew heavily on an important source, Sidney's *Arcadia*, is entirely additional to Painter's account, where the Duchess's imprisonment is very briefly described, without any detail; Ferdinand's wolf-madness, for which Webster used material from Simon Goulart's *Admirable Histories* (1607) translated by Edward Grimeston, is new, and so too the deaths of the brothers and of Antonio. The sub-plot of Julia is an addition, with Castruchio, in the source a Cardinal, conveniently transformed into her husband. Perhaps the most crucial change of all is in Bosola, who in Painter does not appear until the final page of the story where, as a known cut-throat, a 'bloody beast' and an 'assured manqueller' he is hired by the Aragonian brothers to dispatch Antonio. The murder is described in a sentence. He then makes his escape without any difficulty, and the narrative draws to a close with a moralistic paragraph on the folly of Antonio and the Duchess in giving way to their love:

You see the miserable discourse of a Princesse loue, that was not very wise, and of a gentleman that had forgotten his estate, which ought to serue for a loking glasse to them which be ouer hardie in making of enterprises, and do not measure their abilitie with the greatnesse of their attemptes.

(quoted from *The Duchess of Malfi*, ed. J. R. Brown, Revels edition, p. 195)

Painter's *The Palace of Pleasure* is obviously the most important source for the play in the sense of providing the characters and the main outlines of the story, but it supplies little in the way of phrasing. For a writer such as Webster, whose quality of poetic intensity is, for many readers and audiences, his most outstanding gift, any traceable inspiration behind the play's language is of almost equal interest. The question of Webster's verbal borrowings has been very fully examined elsewhere (especially in the works by Boklund and Dent, mentioned in the Suggested Reading) and it is not possible or appropriate to go into detail here, but there are two writers in particular whose philosophical manner and brilliant literary expression had a conspicuous influence on the style of *The Duchess of Malfi*. One is John Florio, whose translation of Montaigne's *Essays* (1603) had great influence on many writers of this period, including Shakespeare; he is a source of proverbial and aphoristic expressions generally, often those with a bitter or cynical tone, and several of Bosola's wry turns of phrase are owed to him. For instance when Antonio twits Bosola by asking if he is studying to become wise, Bosola goes one better in the exchange with a witty riposte based on Montaigne:

> O sir, the opinion of wisdom is a foul tetter, that runs all over a man's body: if simplicity direct us to have no evil, it directs us to a happy being. For the subtlest folly proceeds from the subtlest wisdom. Let me be simply honest.

> (II.i.81–5)

This speech, which is derived from three sentences from separate pages of Florio's Montaigne, *Essays* II, xii, shows Webster's skill in conflating individual lines and phrases into a seamless whole. Webster used this essay ('An Apologie of Raymond Sebond') for another speech of Bosola's in this scene, providing his reductive vision of the essential sameness of all ranks of society:

> Some would think the souls of princes were brought forth by some more weighty cause, than those of meaner persons: they are deceiv'd, there's the same hand to them: the like passions sway them; the same reason, that makes a vicar go to law for a tithe-pig, and undo his neighbours, makes them spoil a whole province, and batter down goodly cities with the cannon.

> (II.i.105–11)

The equivalent passage from Montaigne goes as follows:

> The soules of Emperours and Coblers are all cast in one same mold. Considering the importance of Princes actions, and their weight, wee perswade our selves, they are brought forth by some as weighty and important causes; we are deceived: They are mooved, stirred and remooved in their motions, by the same springs and wardes, that we are in ours. The same reason that makes us chide and braule, and fall out with anie of our neighbours, causeth a warre to follow between Princes; the same reason that makes us whippe or beate a lackey, maketh a Prince (if he apprehend it) to spoyle and waste a whole Province.

> (*Essays*, II.xii)

Webster had, of course, used Florio's Montaigne in a similar sort of way in *The White Devil*, where, as one might expect, he supplies many phrases and ideas for Flamineo's speeches. But his other source was new to *The Duchess of Malfi* and, perhaps because he only read it after he had already begun to write the play, it is not influential until the second half. This is Sidney's *Arcadia*, another work of seminal importance for the Elizabethan age. Although Webster used it in several ways, for general aphorisms, for Julia's dialogues with Bosola and the Cardinal in V.ii, as well as for some of the passionate dialogues between the Duchess and Ferdinand or Bosola, it is in these latter and particularly in debates on virtue and suffering that *Arcadia* leaves its unique traces. When Ferdinand enters the Duchess's chamber in the dark in III.ii and takes her by surprise in her preparations for bed his tone of almost religious horror at her lapse, as at a fall from perfection, is Sidney's:

> Virtue, where art thou hid? What hideous thing
> Is it that doth eclipse thee? . . .
> Or is it true, thou art but a bare name,
> And no essential thing? . . .
> O most imperfect light of human reason,
> That mak'st us so unhappy, to foresee
> What we can least prevent.
> . . . there's in shame no comfort,
> But to be past all bounds and sense of shame.
>
> (III.ii.72–82)

These lines are all to be found in close conjunction in an impassioned soliloquy in *Arcadia* II.i, and Webster has altered them very little, except in the interests of rhythm. Sidney's influence is particularly important also in III.v, in the expressions of grief and suffering given to Antonio and the Duchess at the moment of their parting, in IV.i, in Bosola's descriptions of the Duchess's suffering in her imprisonment and in her own awareness of suffering, in IV.ii, at the beginning and end of the scene, and in the concluding lines of the play. Bosola's beautiful speech at the beginning of IV.i, where he characterizes the Duchess's stoic behaviour in adversity, is dramatically of the greatest importance since it not only confirms the growth of her spirit through suffering which gives this part of the play both its nobility and its pathos, but also expresses a new aspect of refinement in the sensibility of Bosola, in preparation for his crucial change of heart. It demonstrates brilliantly how Webster could take phrases from different parts of his source, perceive the emotional unity between them, and integrate them completely in his own dramatic context. Ferdinand begins the scene asking after the Duchess's bearing in captivity. Bosola gives a set speech in reply:

> She's sad, as one long us'd to't: and she seems
> Rather to welcome the end of misery

> Than shun it: a behaviour so noble,
> As gives a majesty to adversity:
> You may discern the shape of loveliness
> More perfect in her tears, than in her smiles;
> She will muse four hours together: and her silence,
> Methinks, expresseth more than if she spake.

> (IV.1.3–10)

These lines derive from three separate short passages in *Arcadia*: 'But Erona sadde indeede, yet like one rather used, then new fallen to sadnesse ... seemed rather to welcome than to shunne that ende of miserie' (II.xxix); 'a behaviour so noble, as gave a majestie to adversitie' (I.ii); and 'to perceive the shape of loveliness more perfectly in woe than in joyfulness' (II.xxix). The first and third come from the same paragraph, but the middle phrase is from a much earlier chapter, and must have lodged in Webster's mind as he read on through the book. Again the changes are not quantitatively large; but the gains in rhythmic effect and sound quality ('discern' for 'perceive', for instance, and 'in her tears, than in her smiles' for 'in woe than in joyfulness') are immeasurable.

Arcadia also influences the language of the play's conclusion. Bosola's famous expression of determinism, 'We are merely the stars' tennis-balls, struck and banded / Which way please them' (V.iv.53–4), is based on a familiar conceit, but the wording comes directly from a passage in *Arcadia* V, which has supplied a similar tone for his dying lines. Sidney's words are:

In such a shadowe, or rather pit of darkness, the wormish mankinde lives, that neither they know how to forsee, nor what to feare: and are but like tenisballs, tossed by the racket of higher powers.

Bosola exclaims:

> O this gloomy world,
> In what a shadow, or deep pit of darkness
> Doth, womanish, and fearful, mankind live?

> (V.v.100–102)

The exact nature of the process that transformed 'wormish' into 'womanish' would be intriguing to know. This is by no means the philosophy of *Arcadia*, but in *The Duchess of Malfi* these expressions of human insignificance and the futility of life resonate back powerfully over the drama. Webster used his sources very selectively, but in such a way that the division between what one might call his 'own' ideas, and his borrowings, is virtually impossible to make.

2. Plot Summary

The act and scene divisions of *The Duchess of Malfi*, unlike those of *The White Devil*, were set out in the first printed text of 1623. The play is distinctly divided into five acts, with important time-gaps between each.

I.i. The first Quarto of the play prints Act I as a single continuous scene, but modern editors often divide it into two after Antonio's couplet at line 82. If this division is accepted, the play begins with a short opening scene, taking place at the court of Malfi, which introduces Antonio, recently returned to Italy after a long absence in France, and his friend Delio. Antonio's admiration for the example of the good order set by the King of France provides a perspective from which to view the court of Malfi. Antonio and Delio stand back as observers of a brief dialogue between Bosola, a malcontent and former servant of the Cardinal, who is looking for re-employment, and the Cardinal, who seems to discourage him.

I.ii. This is a continuation of the previous scene at court. It is a long, complex scene in several stages, and the diversity of its action well illustrates the unlocalized nature of the Jacobean stage, since Webster is able to move easily, without any break in continuity, from a large-scale public scene in the presence-chamber between Ferdinand, Duke of Calabria, and his courtiers, to an intimate encounter between two characters, observed unseen by a third, which culminates in a private marriage ceremony. Antonio and Delio initially continue in their role as observers, Antonio providing both Delio and the audience with character-sketches of the main participants in the scene. Ferdinand, the Cardinal's brother, is introduced, a mercurial and unbalanced Prince whose unpredictable behaviour is intended to confuse his courtiers about his real intentions. The Duchess, their widowed sister, is, on the other hand, an example of chastity and virtue for court ladies to imitate, according to Antonio's account. The Cardinal urges Ferdinand to employ Bosola as a spy, though he does not wish to be known as Bosola's employer himself. Ferdinand then hires Bosola to spy on the Duchess, and especially to gather information about any possible marriage plans she may have. Bosola dislikes his commission, but accepts it, along with the reward of a post at court. Once alone with their sister, Ferdinand and the Cardinal impress on her their strong desire for her not to remarry. But she has other ideas, and after summoning Antonio to her presence by the pretence that she wishes him to work on her household accounts (he is technically employed as steward of her household), she asks him to be her husband. Cariola, her maid-servant, is a secret witness to the encounter, having been placed by the Duchess behind the arras, so that she can validate the marriage-vow.

II.i. This scene takes place about nine months after the last one. It opens with a satirical dialogue between Bosola and Castruchio, a foolish old man ambitious to become an eminent courtier. They are joined by an old lady who turns out subsequently to be the Duchess's midwife; her presence gives Bosola a cue to express his disgust with human vanity. Antonio enters, followed by the Duchess, attempting to conceal the fact that she is heavily pregnant. Bosola is clearly antagonistic towards Antonio, and he suspects the Duchess to be pregnant though he knows nothing of her marriage. To test his suspicions he offers her apricots, which bring on premature labour, and she is hastily removed from the scene.

II.ii. In this, a night scene which follows soon after, Bosola attempts to detain the old midwife who is anxious to be off to her work, Antonio contrives to have all the Duchess's servants locked in their rooms on the pretence that all are under suspicion for a robbery. In reality he wants them out of the way while the Duchess gives birth. At the end of the scene Cariola announces to Antonio the birth of a son.

II.iii. During the same night, Bosola, prowling about the court, runs into Antonio who is angry and suspicious to see him at large. In making a hasty departure Antonio drops a paper on which is written the horoscope for the new baby. Bosola is delighted with this find, and looks forward to discovering the identity of the baby's father.

II.iv. The scene changes to Rome where the Cardinal is closeted with his mistress Julia, Castruchio's wife. Castruchio's arrival in Rome is announced, with news for Ferdinand, clearly of the Duchess's baby. Delio too arrives, and wooes Julia, who rebuffs him.

II.v. The Cardinal and Ferdinand react to the news that their sister has given birth to a baby. Both are violently incensed, but Ferdinand's passionate outbursts appear excessive even to his brother. They determine on some action of vengeance against her, its nature as yet unspecified.

III.i. This scene takes place at Malfi several years later, in which space of time, we are promptly informed, the Duchess has given birth to two more children. Antonio tells Delio of the anxieties of his situation and of the Duchess's loss of reputation amongst the common people. Ferdinand enters to propose a husband for his sister, and then to question

Bosola. He is now extremely impatient to learn the identity of the Duchess's lover, and plans to confront her in person.

III.ii. This scene follows shortly after, and takes place at night. The Duchess is preparing for bed, talking informally with Antonio and Cariola the while. To tease her, they creep secretly out of the room and when they are gone Ferdinand enters from behind and takes his sister by surprise. She tells him she is married, but he refuses either to see her husband or to hear his name. He departs, vowing never to see her again and leaving her with a poniard. Antonio and Cariola realize with horror that their life of secrecy is now at an end, and the Duchess prepares a plan for Antonio's escape. When Bosola enters to announce that Ferdinand has taken horse for Rome in rage, the Duchess pretends that this is on account of Antonio's mal-administration and dishonesty as steward of her wealth, and publicly dismisses him from her service. At first both Bosola and her servants seem to be taken in by the trick, but when Bosola makes a show of sympathy for Antonio, the Duchess is in turn deceived into revealing to him that Antonio is her husband. Bosola suggests she feign a pilgrimage to Loretto in order to escape the court and join up with Antonio, and she adopts his plan. But he, of course, prepares to disclose all of this to Ferdinand.

III.iii. In a short scene ostensibly chiefly concerned with the departure of the Cardinal and some of the courtiers to war to fight for the Holy Roman Emperor, Bosola arrives and the reactions of Ferdinand and the Cardinal to his latest news about the Duchess are presented.

III.iv. The scene shifts to the shrine of Loretto. A dumbshow is performed in which first the Cardinal, having put off his robes of holy office, is invested with arms as a soldier, and then he enacts a ceremony of ritual banishment of Antonio, the Duchess and their children. Two pilgrims interpret and comment on these actions, providing the important information that because the Pope has been informed by the Cardinal of the 'looseness' of the Duchess's behaviour, he has exercised supreme ecclesiastical authority in depriving her of all her lands and possessions. She and Antonio are now impoverished and powerless.

III.v. Antonio and the Duchess react to their realization of their new situation. Bosola comes with a letter from Ferdinand summoning Antonio to his presence, which the Duchess at once interprets as a threat of death. The couple decide to separate, and Antonio departs with the eldest child to Milan. An armed guard arrives to escort the Duchess back to her palace.

IV.i. The Duchess is now imprisoned in her palace, and Ferdinand embarks on a long process of torturing her. He comes to her in total darkness, in fulfilment of his vow never to see her again, and presents her with a severed hand, supposedly cut from Antonio's body. She is also shown figures of her husband and children which she is led to believe are their corpses, though as Ferdinand makes clear to Bosola and the audience they are only waxen effigies. The Duchess is not cowed by this grotesque action of Ferdinand, but she longs desperately to die. Ferdinand plans further tortures, though Bosola now begins to feel pity for her and begs his master to relent.

IV.ii. In this, one of the play's longest scenes, the Duchess meets her death. She and Cariola, confined in prison-like conditions within her palace, are confronted with a bizarre entertainment presented by the madmen whom Ferdinand has installed next to their lodging. Bosola comes on as part of this weird masque, disguised as an old man. He has come to prepare the Duchess for death, claiming first to be a tomb-maker then the bellman who tolls for condemned prisoners on the night before their execution. He summons executioners who strangle first the Duchess then Cariola. The Duchess's young children are strangled offstage, and their bodies brought on. Ferdinand is overcome with horror and passionate remorse at the sight of his sister's body, which he can hardly bear to look at; he refuses to pay Bosola for his services and instead blames him for the murder. He begins to show signs of madness. Bosola, left alone, bitterly regrets the deed and attempts hopelessly to revive the Duchess. She returns to consciousness for a brief moment, then dies. In a new frame of mind Bosola departs for Milan, intending to join up with Antonio.

V.i. The scene shifts to Milan. Antonio witnesses an encounter between the Marquis of Pescara, on whom lands taken from him and the Duchess have been conferred, and various petitioners. The Marquis refuses to grant this land to Delio, who begs for it on Antonio's behalf, but confers it instead on Julia when she asks for it. He explains to Delio that as wrongfully gained land it should not be awarded to an honest man. Thus Antonio perceives that he still has allies. He plans to pay an unexpected visit to the Cardinal at midnight, in the hope of surprising him into a reconciliation.

V.ii. The courtiers witness the madness of Ferdinand, which the doctor tries ineffectually to cure. The Cardinal makes up an excuse for it, and also pretends to Bosola that he knows nothing of the Duchess's death; he commissions Bosola to kill Antonio. Julia, despite being the Cardinal's mistress, falls in love with Bosola and offers to prove her feelings by performing some service for him. He instructs her to question the Cardinal about the causes of his present melancholy condition, and she arranges for him to spy on the conversation, unseen. The Cardinal, swearing Julia to secrecy on a book, confesses to the murder of the Duchess and her children. The book is poisoned and Julia dies. Bosola, who now knows the Cardinal's involvement in the murder, steps forward to confront him. The Cardinal arranges for Bosola to visit him at midnight to help dispose of Julia's body, intending then to kill him. In a soliloquy at the end of the scene Bosola vows to save Antonio from his enemies, and, if possible, to join with him in revenge.

V.iii. Antonio, wandering with Delio in a cloister close by the Cardinal's lodging, hears an echo, which reminds him of the Duchess's voice, warning him of death.

V.iv. The Cardinal contrives that none of the courtiers shall sit up with Ferdinand, claiming that their presence exacerbates his madness, and makes them promise to keep well away from his lodging, even if they should hear noises. He may produce a false alarm, he says, to test their obedience. In the darkness Bosola arrives to keep his appointment with the Cardinal. Ferdinand, on the prowl, and Antonio, visiting the Cardinal as he had earlier planned, converge on the same spot. In the nocturnal confusion Bosola, intending to kill Ferdinand, whose voice he has recognized, strikes Antonio dead by mistake.

V.v. Bosola comes to kill the Cardinal, bearing Antonio's body with him. The Cardinal's cries for help are heard by the courtiers, but they keep their promise and do not intervene to save him. Ferdinand enters amid the melée and strikes Bosola, who kills him. The Cardinal dies, soon followed by Bosola. The play ends with the appearance of Delio and Antonio's eldest son, who has survived the holocaust. Delio intends to establish him as his mother's heir.

3. Structure

The structure of *The Duchess of Malfi* has been described by the nineteenth-century critic William Archer as 'broken-backed' on account of the long gap of time that elapses between the action of Acts II and III. That more than two years have passed is quickly made known to the audience at the beginning of Act III in the simplest way possible, by having Antonio inform Delio, who has been absent from the court, that the Duchess has produced two more children in the meantime. Delio remarks, 'Methinks 'twas yesterday,' thus expressing on the audience's behalf a sense of the unreality of these years, and the moment passes. In fact the play is rather conspicuously divided into five units with a time-gap signalled between each act, so that the space between Acts II and III is only different from the others by being longer. Act I, though often divided into two parts, consists of a long continuous scene in the court at Malfi, the main action of which is the contracting of a clandestine marriage between the Duchess and Antonio. Act II takes place probably about nine months later; the time-gap is signalled first by a brief expository dialogue between Delio and Antonio:

DELIO: And so long since married?
You amaze me.
ANTONIO: Let me seal your lips for ever,
For did I think that anything but th' air
Could carry these words from you, I should wish
You had no breath at all.

(II.i.5–9)

The main event of this act is the birth of a child to the Duchess and Antonio. The last three acts of the play, separated in time from the first two, depict events which follow swiftly one from another, and are more crowded with incident. In Act III the revelation of the identity of the Duchess's lover to her brothers leads directly to their projects for revenge against her. In this central section of the play the Duchess's secret domestic life with her husband is brought to a sudden end; the ritual scene of banishment at the shrine of Loretto, where the couple have fled for refuge, is followed by the pathetic and moving scene of their parting, never to meet again. Once more, a time-gap is indicated in the opening dialogue of Act IV:

FERDINAND: How doth our sister Duchess bear herself
In her imprisonment?
BOSOLA: Nobly: I'll describe her.
She's sad, as one long us'd to't; and she seems
Rather to welcome the end of misery
Than shun it.

(IV.i.1–5)

This act centres on the brothers' revenge on the Duchess, her torture, suffering and death; it all takes place in her palace at Malfi. Revenge on Antonio is reserved for later, and though Antonio's fate is very much in the background in these scenes, we are not allowed entirely to forget him. Ferdinand informs Bosola at the end of IV.i. that 'Antonio / lurks about Milan', and his death is planned in due course; the Duchess's dying thoughts are for her husband, and Bosola comforts her with a lie before death:

> He's reconcil'd to your brothers: the Pope hath wrought
> The atonement.
>
> (IV.ii.350–1)

This is immediately taken up at the end of the last act, which opens with a discussion between Antonio and Delio as to the possibility of reconciliation with the Duchess's brothers, Antonio not of course yet knowing of his wife's fate. The last scenes all take place in Milan, where Antonio has gone for refuge. Although Bosola has experienced a change of heart and now hopes to preserve Antonio from the brothers' revenge, he must still act secretly and alone. He has no opportunity to make use of the knowledge he has acquired during his career of spying against the masters he had formerly served, and events – the murderous machinations of the Cardinal, Ferdinand's madness, Antonio's independent plotting – so conspire against him that in the end, in the confusion of darkness, he kills Antonio, the very man he had intended to preserve.

The structure of the play, then, though it cannot be said to be tautly organized, is a coherent one, and not as haphazardly planned as some critics have suggested.

It is in some ways clearer to understand than that of *The White Devil*, particularly since the moral status of the main characters is less ambiguous. The Duchess and Antonio, although not admirable or good in a simple way, are by no means 'glorious villains' like Vittoria and Brachiano, and by contrast with them the Duchess's brothers are unequivocally evil. Bosola's crucial change of allegiance in the course of the action is clearly signalled; he begins as tool-villain in the service of Ferdinand and the Cardinal, but undergoes a complete conversion after the Duchess's death and in the last act operates against his former masters. The major events of the play stem from a single act and its consequences – the secret marriage of the Duchess to Antonio, which so enrages her brothers that they seek the ultimate revenge against the couple. With the Duchess's death the revenge is half-accomplished; Ferdinand's madness, Bosola's change of heart and Julia's counter-plotting combine in the last act to complicate the pursuit of revenge against Antonio, so that in the end everyone involved dies. This action accounts for most of the play's content, but since Webster is also concerned to provide the play with a richly textured background of ideas in which the vision of life implied in the presentation of events is expressed more discursively he includes a few scenes which function largely to do this rather than further the plot. Such scenes as the opening of Act 1, for instance, where Antonio and Delio discuss first the French court, and then the main personages in the court at Malfi, or the dialogue between Bosola, Castruchio and the Old

Lady at the beginning of II.i operate in this way. The vestigial sub-plot centred on Julia's liaison with the Cardinal is clearly meant to provide an implicitly contrasting style of secret sexual relationship to that of the Duchess and Antonio; it is linked up with the main plot through Julia's infatuation with Bosola.

This relatively straightforward structure is filled out and enriched by a pattern of parallels and contrasts between the characters. The first comparison to suggest itself is that between the natures of the Duchess's two brothers. Webster draws his audience's attention to it by having Antonio, who has evidently taken on the role of commentator, give character studies of the two brothers in answer to a request for information from Delio:

Now sir, your promise: what's that Cardinal? I mean his temper?

(I.ii.75–6)

When Antonio has given a ten-line portrait of the Cardinal, Delio then halts him: 'You have given too much of him: what's his brother?' The brothers are alike in maintaining appearances which belie their inner natures, and, says Antonio, twins 'In quality'. The Cardinal seems outwardly to be a worldly, sociable man, but inwardly 'is a melancholy churchman. The spring in his face is nothing but the engend'ring of toads' (I.ii.81–3); Ferdinand is 'a most perverse and turbulent nature':

> What appears in him mirth, is merely outside,
> If he laugh heartily, it is to laugh
> All honesty out of fashion.

(I.ii.95–7)

Both are sinister, unscrupulous men operating in the world by undercover methods, and utilizing their courtly power in entirely selfish and corrupt ways. Antonio proceeds to contrast them totally with their sister:

> You never fix'd your eye on three fair medals,
> Cast in one figure, of so different temper.

(I.ii.113–14)

That Antonio's portrait of the Duchess is not entirely disinterested is implied by Delio's amused comment: 'Fie Antonio, / You play the wiredrawer with her commendations.' Nonetheless, as the play goes on to demonstrate, the contrast is an accurate one. But the brothers are less similar than Antonio's account suggests, and although they unite to counsel her jointly against remarriage (I.ii.216–51), their responses in II.v to the discovery that she has given birth to a baby are markedly dissimilar. While the Cardinal is angered at this stain to their family honour he contains his emotions in terse expressions of distaste; he tries unsuccessfully to curb Ferdinand's violent outbreak of passion: 'Speak lower,' 'Why do you make yourself / So wild a tempest?' 'You fly beyond your reason,' 'Are you stark mad?' Ferdinand's emotions are incomprehensible to him and, though by no means explicable to the audience, do at least suggest a complexity of feeling which makes him the more interesting and sympathetic character. From this point on the fates of the brothers diverge, and they only appear together again briefly before the last act. While Ferdinand involves himself personally in punishing his sister by mental and physical torture before having her put to death, the Cardinal operates at a distance, issuing an edict of banishment on the couple, and hiring spies to work for him. Although they die within moments of one another, there is also an element of contrast in their ultimate fates; the passionate Ferdinand goes mad and believes himself an animal, grovelling on the ground, tormentedly aware of the bestial natures of those around him:

Hence, hence, you are all of you like beasts for sacrifice, there's nothing left of you, but tongue and belly, flattery and lechery.

(V.ii.78–81)

His last words recall the passionate attachment which has ruined him:

My sister. O! my sister, there's the cause on't.
Whether we fall by ambition, blood, or lust,
Like diamonds, we are cut with our own dust.

(V.v.71–3)

The calculating Cardinal on the other hand, having poisoned his mistress Julia, meets his death in isolation when the courtiers assume his cries for help to be feigned. His dying words serve, as is usual in Webster, for an appropriate epitaph:

now, I pray let me
Be laid by, and never thought of.

(V.v.89–90)

Just as important contrasts are drawn between the characters of the three members of the high-born family who dominate this play, so too there is a significant relationship between the two major lower-born characters, who in their different ways serve the Aragonian brethren, Antonio and Bosola. Both have recently returned to court after an absence, Antonio in France, Bosola having served seven years as a galley-slave for murder; Antonio has found a position as the grand master of the Duchess's household, a steward like Malvolio, while Bosola, though he has acquired an identity at court as 'the only court-gall', is looking for employment. His position is more ambiguous; the Cardinal has used his services in the past but because of his reputation no longer wishes to be publicly associated with him. None the less, he recognizes Bosola's abilities as a spy and urges Ferdinand to hire him, although, significantly, Ferdinand would prefer Antonio (I.ii.148–53); but the Cardinal is the better judge of character, and dismisses Ferdinand's suggestion;

> You are deceiv'd in him,
> His nature is too honest for such business.
>
> (I.i.153–4)

Bosola then undertakes Ferdinand's commission, although he is aware of the nature of the work in store for him and initially reluctant to involve himself in it. His moral objections to accepting Ferdinand's offer of money to spy on the Duchess are not abandoned when Ferdinand offers him a token post at court in addition, but in a strange way he is now able to agree to the business. He takes a bitter pleasure in joking about the appropriateness of the post:

> what's my place?
> The provisorship o'th' horse? say then my corruption
> Grew out of horse-dung. I am your creature.
>
> (I.ii.209–11)

The careers of the two men are implicitly compared from the first. Antonio is rejected as a possible servant for Ferdinand and the Cardinal, Bosola chosen instead. The scene in which Bosola is appointed to an official position, albeit a rather lowly one, at court is followed by a scene in which Antonio is also promoted, in a different but also equivocal kind of way. Soon after, the two men have their first confrontation, a brief, edgy scene with both consciously sparring for advantage; each twits the other with his preferment, Bosola ironically entitling Antonio 'lord of the ascendant, chief man with the Duchess' (II.i.100–101). When they meet again in the darkness outside the Duchess's lodging, on the night when she gives birth, the antagonism between them is open. Bosola is jealous of Antonio's success at court, Antonio defensively aware that the other is spying on him. Each knows that the other's status is his weak point:

BOSOLA: You are a false steward.
ANTONIO: Saucy slave! I'll pull thee up by the roots.
BOSOLA: Maybe the ruin will crush you to pieces.

> (II.iii.35–7)

Appropriately, it is by pretending sympathy for Antonio that Bosola gets the Duchess to reveal her secret marriage; in this scene (III.ii) he claims to believe that virtue matters more than noble blood, but later he discloses his true feelings about Antonio, urging the Duchess to 'Forget this base, low fellow ... One of no birth' (III.v). Antonio seeks, as a servant, to better himself but he is not unaware of the dangers that attend ambition; he allows himself in the wooing scene to be overcome by the Duchess's ardour into agreeing to marriage although he never for a moment forgets the difference in their social positions, and the difficulties these create for her as much as for him. But this is a world which will not accept stewards who marry their mistresses: the pilgrims at Loretto, who function as objective commentators, pity Antonio and his helplessness against the power of the Aragonian brothers, but none the less recognize the social impossibility of the marriage:

> Here's a strange turn of state: who would have thought
> So great a lady would have match'd herself
> Unto so mean a person?
>
> (III.iv.23–5)

Once Antonio is separated from the Duchess and no longer sheltered by her secret protection, he feels his life is worthless; his plan to take the Cardinal by surprise in a midnight confrontation (V.i.61–73) is a desperate enterprise which he knows from the start is doomed to fail. But it will at least put an end to a life without real identity:

> Yet it shall rid me of this infamous calling,
> For better fall once, then be ever falling.
>
> (V.i.72–3)

Bosola, by a different route, is equally disillusioned with a life of service. R. Ornstein, in *The Moral Vision of Jacobean Tragedy*, calls Antonio and Bosola 'brothers under the skin ... who committed spiritual suicide'. Rejected by Ferdinand once the murder of the Duchess has been accomplished, Bosola realizes that he has damned himself for nothing, not even for the reward of his master's approval. In committing himself to Ferdinand, he has made a fatal error in his choice of allegiance:

> ... though I loath'd the evil, yet I lov'd
> You that did counsel it; and rather sought
> To appear a true servant than an honest man.
>
> (IV.ii.329–31)

But in his effort to switch to serving Antonio he fares no better; his attempt to befriend the man who was once both his victim and rival leads directly to Antonio's death, during the confusion in the dark when he strikes Antonio in mistake for the Cardinal. The two men are drawn together in a final contrast. For Antonio this death is the answer to a life-long petition: 'Thou hast ended a long suit, / In a minute' (V.iv.46–7). Antonio's death constitutes a surrender to the futility of 'the quest of greatness', but Bosola has some satisfaction in his final moments, giving the death blow to both Ferdinand and the Cardinal: 'the last part of my life / Hath done me best service' (V.v.64–5). 'Thou hast thy payment too,' comments the Cardinal wryly, for Bosola has been given a fatal wound by Ferdinand, but he has at least the pleasure of achieving his revenge: 'It may be pain, but no harm to me to die / In so good a quarrel' (V.v.99–100).

The relationship of these two characters is a central structural feature of the play, drawing together the major themes of service and the relationships of masters and servants, and giving point and coherence to the play's last act. The contrast between the Duchess and Julia is much less integral to the total effect, and only intermittently significant, but it does again serve the purpose of drawing together themes in the play. Julia has only three appearances altogether, with the Cardinal and Delio in II.iv, and with the courtiers, the Cardinal and Bosola in V.i and ii. Like the Duchess, she is involved in a sexual relationship which must be kept secret, though for very different reasons, since it is not only adulterous but also with the Cardinal. This liaison, like that of Antonio and the Duchess, casts a fresh light on the conventional moral values of the court of Malfi. Like the Duchess, too, Julia is a woman in a man's world; she thinks herself a 'great woman of pleasure' (V.ii.190) who can choose and reject amongst potential suitors at will, and she enjoys the idea of reversing sexual roles by soliciting Bosola. She takes up the play's conspicuous strain of jewellery images, applying the idea to the man she lusts for rather than, as would be more conventional, to a woman:

> If I see, and steal a diamond,
> The fault is not i'th' stone, but in me the thief
> That purloins it.

(V.ii.187–9)

But her power is only an illusion; where she believes herself to be the aggressor with Bosola, even pointing a pistol at him, he is in fact using her to extract secrets from the Cardinal. In V.i Pescara presents her with land when she asks for it, but only because the land itself was first obtained by corruption, being stolen from Antonio, and he thinks it 'a gratification / Only due to a strumpet'. It has been suggested that Webster meant Delio's overtures to her in II.iv to be only a preliminary to using her as a means of gaining information about Antonio's enemies, as Francisco uses Zanche in *The White Devil*, which is plausible although there is no evidence for it. Her status as would-be deceiver deceived is aptly symbolized in the manner of her death, poisoned by kissing a holy book whose significance as a pledge of truth she had in any case intended to betray. She is an evil obverse to the Duchess, but like her in that she has the illusion, but not the reality of power, and all her efforts to use her power for pleasure only end in her own destruction.

The ending of the play makes a gesture towards the affirmation of positive values in the constitution of a new social order, which is conventional at the conclusion of a tragic play, but in several ways this seems to be only a token. The deaths in the last scenes are brought about in an atmosphere of confusion and misunderstanding. Nothing goes according to plan. Bosola kills Antonio, the man he meant to save. The Cardinal's cries for help are mistaken by his supporters for counterfeiting. In the dark mad Ferdinand strikes out indiscriminately. Ferdinand wounds Bosola, Bosola kills the Cardinal and Ferdinand, then dies himself. The Cardinal's supporters come on the scene too late. At the last moment Delio makes an entry with a new character, hardly seen before, the eldest son of Antonio and the Duchess. The sole survivor of his ill-fated family, this child who has been born and has grown up in the course of the play's action, is established by the upright Delio as the hope of the future. Is this a new beginning? Delio's imagery implies that the past can be wiped out:

> These wretched eminent things
> Leave no more fame behind 'em, than should one
> Fall in a frost, and leave his print in snow;
> As soon as the sun shines, it ever melts
> Both form and matter.

(V.v.113–17)

With his dying breath the child's father has wished that his son may 'fly the courts of princes', yet Delio has deliberately brought him back to reclaim his inheritance. Hints of affirmation do not prevail over a dominant tone of fatalism, but they are not wholly absent.

4. Imagery and Dramatic Language

Most of the generalizations about the imagery of the *White Devil* apply equally well to *The Duchess of Malfi*. The language of the play is just as rich in evocative metaphors and various kinds of figurative language, and the same sources of imagery predominate, especially animals, poison and disease, light and dark, storms, jewels and the diabolic. If anything, the imagery of this play expresses a more consistently pessimistic view of human life than *The White Devil*, despite the more distinctive presence of virtuous characters, and a gesture towards a new order at the end.

The play is particularly rich in images of animal life, which are used both in relation to individual characters, and more generally to convey a view of life in which human behaviour has little to distinguish it from the bestial. A wide range of animals and birds are mentioned, including dogs, caterpillars, blackbirds, crows, magpies, horse-leeches, horses, toads, dormice, crabs, lampreys, pigeons, goats, lice, worms, hedgehogs, pigs and especially wolves. Bosola's description of the status of the Cardinal and Ferdinand as Princes in relation to their dependents not only expresses his own cynicism about great men but also, in conjunction with the other dominant strains of figurative language in the play, a wider attitude:

He and his brother are like plum trees, that grow crooked over standing pools, they are rich, and o'erladen with fruit, but none but crows, pies, and caterpillars feed on them. Could I be one of their flatt'ring panders, I would hang on their ears like a horse-leech, till I were full, and then drop off.

(I.i.49–54)

In some ways, Bosola goes on to say, men who depend on princes' favours are worse off than hawks or dogs, since these creatures get some reward for their service, when human retainers may well end up as despised outcasts. The life of service is the subject of another of his vigorous figurative expressions; in III.ii he refers dismissively to the officers who slander Antonio when they believe him fallen, using an image of that animal which, to many writers of this period, symbolized both oppression and pitiable dependency, the bear:

> These are rogues, that in's prosperity,
> But to have waited on his fortune, could have wish'd
> His dirty stirrup riveted through their noses:
> And follow'd after's mule, like a bear in a ring.

(III.ii.228–31)

The reduction of the human to the bestial is a constant theme. Bosola cites the lady of France who out of vanity has the pock-marked skin of her face flayed off to make it smoother, 'and whereas before she look'd like a nutmeg grater, after she resembled an abortive hedgehog' (II.i. 31–2). The Old Lady's closet of cosmetics is said to contain such items as the fat of serpents and the spawn of snakes; the human body is consumed by diseases with animals' names 'as the most ulcerous wolf, and swinish measle' (II.i.58) and 'eaten up of lice, and worms'. It is not only Bosola who sees life in this way. Ferdinand's mind is obsessed by animality, and the discovery that his sister has taken a lover unleashes from him a torrent of bestial fantasy. The sound of her voice is like the cry of a screech-owl, and more horrifying than a wolf's howling (III.i.90); her laughter is that of a hyena (II.v.39); her children are cubs or young wolves; her lover should be punished by being locked up with only dogs, monkeys and other dumb creatures for company. The wolf increasingly dominates his imagination, and becomes an image for himself; his lycanthropia in the last act enables him to express in violent ravings truths which would be unacceptable from the mouths of the sane:

Hence, hence! you are all of you like beasts for sacrifice, there's nothing left of you, but tongue and belly, flattery and lechery.

The savage wolf, whose cry is a howl of torment, is an apt transformation for the deranged Ferdinand. Other wild animals who prey for livelihood on weaker creatures, such as the tiger or the fox, are also related to Ferdinand and his brother. Conversely, the creature who is defenceless against the depredations of nature's bloodlust is represented by the bird, who, as in *The White Devil*, figures in several expressions of human vulnerability. The bird's characteristic element is the freedom of the air, and to the Duchess 'the birds that live i' th' field / On the wild benefit of nature' are luckier than she, in that they are at liberty to choose their own mates; but the caged bird, like the Duchess in her confinement, cannot survive (IV.ii.12). Bosola in one of his meditations likens the soul in the body to a caged bird:

Did'st thou ever see a lark in a cage? such is the soul in the body: this world is like her little turf of grass, and the heaven o'er our heads, like her looking-glass, only gives us a miserable knowledge of the small compass of our prison.

(IV.ii.128–32)

Elsewhere in contemporary literature this image is given a hopeful connotation, as for instance in Spenser's *The Faerie Queene*, VI, canto vi, where the imprisonment in the cage is seen as merely a temporary condition preliminary to a permanent state of freedom after death, but Bosola's words emphasize only the miseries of life on earth. The Duchess and Antonio are also like 'silly birds' lured into a trap or 'pheasants and quails', preserved alive only till they are fat enough for eating. The idea of human beings as victims allowed a measure of liberty and even self-assertion but only as long as it suits the whims of those in power, is embodied in the situation of the Duchess in the hands of her brothers; on a smaller scale, the relationship of Julia to the Cardinal, and the imagery Webster gives to the Cardinal to express his sense of it, make the same point. The Cardinal, sardonically relishing his control over Julia, welcomes her to Rome:

> You may thank me, lady,
> I have taken you off your melancholy perch,
> Bore you upon my fist, and show'd you game,
> And let you fly at it. I pray thee kiss me.
> When thou wast with thy husband, thou wast watch'd
> Like a tame elephant: (still you are to thank me.)
> Thou hadst only kisses from him, and high feeding,
> But what delight was that?

> (II.iv.27–34)

Although the Cardinal contrasts his own treatment of Julia favourably with that of her husband, in fact there is little real difference; for the one she is 'a tame elephant', an exotic pet to be prized and pampered, for the other a hawk, who may be given the opportunity to fly at game, but is none the less kept tied to its owner's fist.

Animals are both predators on human life, and victims of it. They are also one means of representing the violence of passion which in this play overcomes human rationality, most particularly, in Ferdinand's lycanthropia, but also in a more general sense of the human incapacity to live a measured and orderly existence according to the precepts of Christianity and humanism in a world so uncontrollably chaotic. The connecting thread between many of the most important strains of imagery is the idea of disorder. It is significant that Antonio's first speech in the play addresses the concept of good government; he admires the French king for his aims and methods in 'seeking to reduce both State and people / To a fix'd order' by ridding his court of flatterers and evil counsellors. The moral identity of a court determines that of its country:

> A Prince's court
> Is like a common fountain, whence should flow

Pure silver-drops in general. But if 't chance
Some curs'd example poison't near the head,
Death and diseases through the whole land spread.

(I.i.11–15)

The imagery Antonio employs here, of poison and disease which infiltrate a whole system and progressively destroy it, also pervades the
play. The life of the court, with its atmosphere of gossip and 'whisper-
ing-rooms', court calumny, 'a pestilent air which princes' palaces /
Are seldom purg'd of', nocturnal revelry, suspicion, political machina-
tion, flattery and deception, is aptly likened by Ferdinand to 'a rank
pasture', which breeds 'a kind of honey-dew that's deadly: / 'Twill
poison your fame' (I.ii.231–2). Bosola is called by Antonio 'the only
court-gall', 'gall' meaning a sore produced by rubbing or chafing, so
that the term itself suggests his activities as a railing satirist who
scratches away at the court's vices until they become inflamed. His
goodness, according to Antonio, is 'poisoned' by his 'foul melancholy'.
His gift of out-of-season apricots to the Duchess when she is pregnant acts on her like poison, and the imagery of poison is connected
with her marriage in other ways too. Cariola, choosing a solemn expression by which to pledge her fidelity to the Duchess's confidence,
vows,

I'll conceal this secret from the world
As warily as those that trade in poison,
Keep poison from their children.

(I.ii.274–6)

But the secret cannot be preserved, and Ferdinand receives the news of
what he at first believes to be his sister's clandestine liaison with a
strange cry of passion: 'I have this night digg'd up a mandrake ... And I
am grown mad with't (II.v.12). The exact meaning of his words is obscure; but the mandrake, a plant which was sometimes said to madden
anyone that pulled it up by giving a shriek, was also poisonous. Ferdinand later tells Bosola that the marriage 'drew a stream of gall quite
through my heart'. 'Gall' here may only mean bitterness, but it could
also mean venom, and the intensity of Ferdinand's reaction to his sister's
marriage is so evidently unnatural as to make the idea that he feels
himself poisoned by it quite appropriate. It would also connect up with
his sense that by acting as she has done the Duchess has shown herself
inherently corrupt, and for Ferdinand this corruption is the more painful
to contemplate in that, as her twin brother, he too must share it. The
Cardinal, the oldest of the three siblings, takes the news of her giving

birth as evidence of sexual looseness, which will, in a conventional way, blemish their family honour:

> Shall our blood?
> The royal blood of Aragon and Castile,
> Be thus attainted?

(II.v.21–3)

He uses 'blood' metaphorically, to mean family relationship and to refer to their high rank. But Ferdinand, in his reply, though also speaking figuratively, extends the idea of tainted blood to the physical plane:

> Apply desperate physic,
> We must not now use balsamum, but fire,
> The smarting cupping-glass, for that's the mean
> To purge infected blood, such blood as hers.

(II.v.23–6)

He imagines purging his sister's blood not by some act of spiritual penitence, but by violence; he will hew her to pieces, burn her body in a charcoal-pit or set fire to her bed. The notion of her beauty co-existing with her impurity enrages him, for each seems to intensify the other:

> Methinks her fault and beauty,
> Blended together, show like leprosy,
> The whiter, the fouler.

(III.iii.61–3)

In Webster's time it was believed that sexual intercourse involved the mingling of blood, hence Ferdinand's horror at the thought of his sister's unsanctified copulation for she has corrupted his own blood as well as hers:

> Damn her! that body of hers,
> While that my blood ran pure in't, was more worth
> Than that which thou would'st comfort, call'd a soul.

(IV.i.119–21)

He refers elsewhere to her 'whore's blood' (II.v.49) and to the 'rank blood' (III.i.78), which has caused her, like the sinister effects of witch-craft, to 'dote on some desertless fellow' (III.i.65). Her love for Antonio is to Ferdinand evidence of inherent corruption, a spotted liver (I.ii.222), a tainted heart.

But the Duchess is by no means the only character associated with ideas of physical impurity. Bosola, in one of his meditations, suggests that life itself is a disease which we fear to cure, since the only remedy is death:

> Though we are eaten up of lice and worms,
> And though continually we bear about us
> A rotten and dead body, we delight
> To hide it in rich tissue: all our fear,
> Nay, all our terror, is lest our physician
> Should put us in the ground, to be made sweet.
>
> (II.i.59–64)

This conception, explicitly set out here by Bosola, though it may not represent the whole truth of the vision which the play has to offer, is none the less forcefully implied at many points in the play; and the fact that several of the characters are made to draw upon images of disease to express other ideas keeps the theme alive throughout. Julia, for instance, describing how the cardinal wooed her, recalls that,

> You told me of a piteous wound i'th' heart,
> And a sick liver, when you wooed me first,
> And spake like one in physic.
>
> (II.iv.37–9)

The Duchess, arguing with Bosola that to curse the stars is not a pointless act just because it does not produce an immediate effect, uses an analogy with disease:

> Plagues, that make lanes through largest families,
> Consume them.
>
> (IV.i.101–102)

So does Antonio, pointing out that no buildings, however strong, endure forever:

> Churches and cities, which have diseases like to men
> Must have like death that we have.
>
> (V.iii.17–18)

Such language reinforces the pervasive theme of decay. Corruption is omnipresent. The Duchess, so pure in Antonio's eyes that 'her very sleeps / Are more in heaven, than other ladies' shrifts' (I.ii.127–8) has tainted blood, and her body, like everyone else's, putrifies daily. Bosola tells her, 'Thou art a box of worm seed, at best, but a salvatory of green mummy', a prison for worms. The Old Lady's closet contains substances such as 'fat of serpents; spawn of snakes, Jews' spittle, and their young children's ordure', and repairing the sins of her youth is enough to make her doctor a wealthy man. Bosola, promoted to office in Ferdinand's household, notes wryly that his 'corruption / Grew out of horse dung'. Appropriately then, death may be seen as only an intensification of the disease of life; and as such, the Duchess does not fear it:

> The apoplexy, catarrh, or cough o'th' lungs
> Would do as much.

> (IV.ii.209–10)

For Antonio, too, life is merely 'this ague' which he will gladly be rid of. This almost medieval sense of *contemptus mundi* is made explicit, again by Bosola who is often the play's mouthpiece for such ideas, in the dirge he recites to the Duchess in his guise as bellman:

> *Of what is't fools make such vain keeping?*
> *Sin their conception, their birth, weeping:*
> *Their life, a general mist of error,*
> *Their death, a hideous storm of terror.*

> (IV.ii.185–8)

Other images of confusion and inversion supplement this general identification of life with horror and death. The Duchess's marriage leads her into a pathless wilderness, and may be evidence of the 'spirit of madness' that reigns in her, according to Cariola; taught the error of her ways, she curses the world 'to its first chaos'. Her murder is a symbol of disorder: 'blood flies upwards, and bedews the heavens.' Afterwards Ferdinand's loss of equilibrium expresses itself in his wolf-madness, which causes him to howl like an animal and prowl churchyards at night, digging up graves. In the play's final two scenes confusion is graphically enacted, when the Cardinal's cries for help are misinterpreted as play-acting by his followers, Antonio is stabbed in the dark in mistake for his enemy, and Bosola, Ferdinand and the Cardinal kill one another. The dying Bosola draws attention to the playwright's conscious use of theatricalism at this point:

MALATESTE: Then wretched thing of blood,
                       How came Antonio by his death?
BOSOLA: In a mist: I know not how;
                Such a mistake as I have often seen
                In a play.

> (V.v.93–6)

This last mistake seems to confirm the vision of futility and hopelessness; 'That we cannot be suffer'd / To do good when we have a mind to it'

(IV.ii.357–8) is apparently the dispiriting conclusion offered, with the implication that such impulses are in any case rare enough.

There are other strains of imagery that reinforce this prevalent conception of cosmic anarchy. References to storms, earthquakes and various kinds of violent upheaval, particularly centring on the Duchess's marriage and its consequences, suggest the ways in which an act can have repercussions completely beyond the control of any individual. When the Duchess tells Antonio, in the scene in which she woos him, that he has yet to discover 'what a wealthy mine / I make you lord of' she intends to suggest that she will bring him riches beyond his expectations; but in fact she connects his destiny with a mine in another sense, in that their marriage renders them desperately exposed to danger and hostility. Later she is to say 'I stand / As if a mine, beneath my feet, were ready / To be blown up' (III.ii.155–7). Antonio sees Bosola as a mole intent on undermining his security (II.iii.13); Ferdinand's rage at the news of his sister's liaison makes him wish he could be a tempest to destroy her:

> That I might toss her palace 'bout her ears,
> Root up her goodly forests, blast her meads,
> And lay her general territory as waste,
> As she hath done her honour's.
>
> (II.v.17–21)

His falsely consoling message of 'love and safety' to her is like 'calm weather / At sea before a tempest' (III.v.24–5). Life is dangerous and unpredictable. Bosola, hoping to redeem the errors of his life in saving Antonio from the Cardinal's revenge, speaks of the 'slippery ice-pavements' he must negotiate (V.ii.330) but, as events show, he stumbles and falls. His sense of impotence against malevolent fortune is vividly expressed, in an image that Webster's audience would have found entirely familiar:

> We are merely the stars' tennis-balls, struck and banded
> Which way please them.
>
> (V.iv.53–4)

References to fortune and the stars suggest that even if life appears to be without pattern or detectable order it is nonetheless not wise to assume responsibility for one's own destiny. The Duchess berates Cariola as a 'superstitious fool' for her objections to the idea of a feigned pilgrimage, but of course the pilgrimage, suggested by Bosola, puts the Duchess directly into the hands of her brothers. Eventually her sufferings induce in her an attitude of humility in the face of circumstance; she speaks both of 'Heaven's scourge-stick' and 'Fortune's wheel' (III.v.78, 93) as symbols of external control exerted over human affairs. Though her last religious reference is to a Christian concept – 'heaven gates are not so highly arch'd / As princes' palaces' – the final impression is one of stoic submission in the face of the unknown.

Antonio is depicted as a man who, although he acknowledges ambition and is persuaded to step outside the norms of conventional behaviour, is by nature law-abiding. By means of several omens or signs of misfortune to come, Webster seems to imply that Antonio has contravened some kind of supernatural injunctions. For instance, when he casts a horoscope for his child – an action that might not be in itself interpretable as superstitious in Jacobean England – he drops the paper and so betrays the Duchess's secret to Bosola. At the same time his nose bleeds, and his very denial that this event has any significance – 'One that were superstitious, would count / This ominous: when it merely comes by chance' (II.iii.42–3) – must operate to suggest to the audience the opposite conclusion. Though he believes that heaven's intervention in human affairs is benevolently manipulative, like a clock-maker attending to a defective mechanism, and chooses to remain sceptical about the implied supernatural warnings of death in the echo scene, his absurdly accidental death brings to him a recognition that his own life has been without aim or meaning:

> In all our quest of greatness,
> Like wanton boys, whose pastime is their care,
> We follow after bubbles, blown in th'air.
>
> (V.iv.63–5)

Verbal imagery and stage action are closely interfused in this play. The most obvious example of this is the way that images relating human to animal behaviour are realized in Ferdinand's transformation into a wolf-man. The metaphor of life as theatre, which is less common in the dialogue but significantly expressed and placed when it does occur, is also embodied in stage action, though in a less direct way. I. S. Ekeblad, in her article 'The Impure Art of John Webster' has noticed that the entry and presentation of the 'wild consort / Of madmen' in IV.ii, who have been sent by Ferdinand to torment his sister, and the subsequent appearance of Bosola in disguise follow the typical structure and pattern of events in a court masque. First comes the anti-masque (originally 'ante-masque') of comic or grotesque characters whose antics precede the main masque. Thus, as the masques are announced to the audience and presented in introductory speeches and songs, so in IV.ii the scene opens with Cariola and the Duchess discussing the hideous noise of madmen outside their lodging, and a servant enters to announce that the madmen are to come in to provide the Duchess with some 'sport'. He lists the varieties represented as if describing the characters in a play:

> There's a mad lawyer, and a secular priest,
> A doctor that hath forfeited his wits
> By jealousy; an astrologian,
> That in his works said such a day o'th' month
> Should be the day of doom; and, failing of't,
> Ran mad ...

(IV.ii.45–50)

The madmen enter, sing a suitable, dirge-like song 'to a dismal kind of music', and then speak some lines of mad and bawdy dialogue. There follows a dance 'with music answerable thereunto', the madmen leave, and the second part of the entertainment, or masque proper, begins with the entry of Bosola 'like an old man'. He represents a symbolic masque character, presumably here Death, for he tells the Duchess he has come to make her tomb, and he brings her a 'present' of 'coffin, cords, and a bell' (I.164–5). Finally he recites a solemn verse bidding the Duchess prepare herself for death; this might well have been intended to seem, to an audience familiar with the conventions of a marriage-masque, like a parodic inversion of the epithalamium with which the piece would end, predicting and celebrating the joys of the wedding night.

Bosola urges the Duchess to,

> Don clean linen, bathe your feet,
> And, the foul fiend more to check,
> A crucifix let bless your neck

(IV.ii.190–2)

as if preparing herself, like a bride, for a solemn rite. The significance of this episode lies in the relationship between marriage and death in the play. A court masque was a specially commissioned royal entertainment devised to celebrate an occasion of rejoicing, especially a marriage, with as much formal splendour as possible. It involved music, song, dance, stage spectacle, as well as dialogue between symbolic personifications, such as Time or Reason, or classical deities. Courtiers, often members of the royal family themselves, participated, and the entertainment would conclude with dancing in which the masquers would descend into the audience to find partners. Recent examples of such productions, which might well have been in Webster's mind, include Jonson's *Hymenaei* (1608), Campion's *The Lords' Masque* (1613) and Beaumont's *Masque of the Inner Temple and Gray's Inn* (1613), the latter two of which were performed to celebrate the wedding of James I's daughter, Princess Elizabeth, to the Elector Palatine.

The conjunction of marriage and death has been suggested earlier in the play in the scene where the Duchess woos Antonio. Here the bantering dialogue, redolent with half-meanings and unspoken thoughts, puns on the familiar but still shocking interaction between the languages of love and of death. The Duchess sends for her steward on the pretext of making her will, to enquire 'What's laid up for tomorrow'; such a task, she says, normally falls to a woman's husband, but since she is a widow she will make Antonio her 'overseer'. The offices of husband and executor are thus equated. And when Antonio advises the Duchess to 'first provide for a good husband' in her will, the two possible meanings, relating either to her dead husband or to a potential second one, make way for a pun on the idea of giving herself, 'In a winding sheet' to the dead husband, or 'In a couple' to the living. Death forms a subject of the exchange, and a sub-text; the Duchess compares her living self with the idea of her dead or dying self, the smiling woman she now is, with the one to come, making a will 'in deep groans, and terrible ghastly looks', the young widow wooing a second husband with 'the figure cut in alabaster / Kneels at my husband's tomb' (I.ii.373–4). The contract between the couple is sealed with words that relate primarily to the idea of Antonio's release from the office of steward but also to death:

> 'cause you shall not come to me in debt,
> Being now my steward, here upon your lips
> I sign your *Quietus est*:

(I.ii.381–3)

'Quietus est', which culminates the series of allusions to death in the dialogue, is a legal phrase, referring to the discharge or acquittal of someone from a payment due, and it is used again in this sense by the Duchess to Antonio at III.ii.187; but of course it can also apply metaphorically to the release of death. Thus the marriage of Antonio and the Duchess is enacted in an atmosphere of foreboding, due both to the circumstances but also to the way the relationship of love and death is expressed in the language. Her death scene is, as J. R. Brown says, 'her brother's celebration of her marriage . . . a royal occasion, a formal and

necessary meeting, a mingling of sensuality, love, religion and art' (*The Duchess of Malfi*, Revels Edition, p. xxxvii).

Action and language also interact through the allusions to and actual use of effigies and waxen images. In the scene just discussed, the Duchess rather shockingly refers to the carved image of herself kneeling at her husband's tomb, recalling a style of funereal monument popular in Jacobean England, where elaborately carved and painted effigies of the spouse and children of the deceased, represented in contemporary costume, would be posed in devotional attitudes round the carved figure of the dead person, who was usually either stretched out at length or perhaps propped up on one elbow. In the Duchess's death scene styles of tomb-making are referred to again when Bosola, in his guise as tomb-maker, satirically describes the latest fashion in effigies:

> Princes' images on their tombs
> Do not lie as they were wont, seeming to pray
> Up to Heaven; but with the hands under their cheeks,
> As if they died of the tooth-ache; they are not carved
> With their eyes fix'd upon the stars; but as
> Their minds were wholly bent upon the world,
> The self-same way they seem to turn their faces.
>
> (IV.ii.155–61)

A moment or two after these words executioners enter with the Duchess's coffin and she is presently strangled and then, presumably, laid in it, where her body rests for her brother's contemplation. It is important in reading these scenes to recall the visual effect of the other effigies and images of death which are present on the stage. In IV.i Ferdinand visits his sister in the dark, and leaves with her what she takes to be the hand cut from the dead body of Antonio, while Bosola, drawing back a curtain or covering over the discovery-space area at the back of the stage, reveals to her a waxen tableau showing, according to the stage direction, 'the artificial figures of Antonio and his children; appearing as if they were dead'. Although the Duchess is deceived by the representation, Bosola's words at this point imply that the figures are unreal, or at least that they belong to art rather than nature:

> Look you: here's the piece from which 'twas tane;
> He doth present you this sad spectacle,
> That now you know directly they are dead.

'Piece' and 'spectacle' are both terms which suggest theatre or symbolic imagery, and seem to connect with the Duchess's reference a few lines later to her picture 'fashion'd out of wax' (IV.i.63). 'Excellent,' says

Ferdinand, 'as I would wish; she's plagu'd in art' (IV.i.110). It seems appropriate to imagine that the effigies of Antonio and the children remain onstage throughout this scene and the next; the references in the text to the conjunction of art and life may be reinforced by this striking representation of the way that one may be taken for the other. Even if the Duchess is tormented only by 'feigned statues' and not real corpses, her suffering is no less; she does not discover the truth until much too late, and in fact Webster seems to be making the point that the revelation matters much more to Bosola than to her.

At the beginning of IV.ii it appears almost as if the life is being drained away from the Duchess, and replaced by an aesthetic quality of life-likeness:

DUCHESS: Who do I look like now?
CARIOLA: Like to your picture in the gallery,
        A deal of life in show, but none in practice.

(IV.ii.30–32)

So it follows quite fittingly that this scene, the masque of madmen, takes its structure from an art-form rather than from any attempt to represent the accidentals of life. In the last two acts of the play the characters are made several times to speak of their own consciousness of behaving like actors. The Duchess feels herself miscast in a play she is forced to perform:

I account this world a tedious theatre,
For I do play a part in't 'gainst my will.

(IV.i.83–4)

Ferdinand sees Bosola as an actor who does not get the recognition he deserves:

For thee, (as we observe in tragedies
That a good actor many times is curs'd
For playing a villain's part) I hate thee for't.

(IV.ii.286–8)

In this instance the actor's art militates against himself, for the more skilfully he plays his part the less the audience can favour him. Bosola's epitaph on himself is that he 'was an actor in the main of all,/Much 'gainst mine own good nature' (V.v.85–6). Art shares the disorder of life. Antonio meets his death in 'such a mistake as I have often seen / In a play' (V.v.95–6). These images reflect on the play's representation of life and its meanings, and on the author's consciousness of how the very form of his play is in itself significant.

5. Themes

Order and Disorder

The primary theme of the play seems almost to announce itself in the opening lines, when Antonio gives the reasons for his admiration of the French court from which he has just returned. The King of France, in aiming for good order in his state, has begun by turning his own court into a model of government, ridding it of flatterers and providing himself with wise counsellors, who will not be afraid to speak freely about corruption. The moral perfection of the court represents divine order in microcosm and relates directly to the moral and spiritual condition of the country. If the court is corrupt, then its corruption will infiltrate and poison the whole land. These are familiar enough concepts, but by expressing them so strongly and placing them prominently at the start of his play Webster makes it clear that what is to follow, since it takes place in the court of Princes, will not be simply a story of private and individual passions, since nothing a Prince does can be without its wider significance. Accordingly, Princes must conduct themselves with a sense of their place and duty since they exist at the head of a hierarchically structured institution, and they must lead their lives with an understanding of how their decisions will impinge on those beneath them. Like the Medici and the Orsini families in *The White Devil*, the Aragonian brothers, Ferdinand and the Cardinal, are heads of a great dynasty; their sister, the Duchess, has her part in this too, as well as being, by the decease of her first husband, the head of her own household at Malfi. The play's first scene demonstrates both the power and the vulnerability of people in such positions. First, a brief encounter between Bosola and the Cardinal is played out, watched by Antonio and Delio, who stand to the side as observers and commentators. Bosola has recently returned from serving a sentence in the galleys as punishment for a crime committed in the Cardinal's service; he is resentfully dependent on the Cardinal, who, it seems, no longer wishes to support him. Antonio notices how the lack of opportunity to further one's career creates dangerous discontents in natures such as Bosola's:

> This foul melancholy
> Will poison all his goodness, for, I'll tell you,
> If too immoderate sleep be truly said
> To be an inward rust unto the soul;
> It then doth follow want of action

> Breeds all black malcontents, and their close rearing,
> Like moths in cloth, do hurt for want of wearing.

(I.i.75–81)

The fact of the Cardinal's powerful influence, for good or evil, over the destiny of his dependents is reinforced by the encounter which follows, between Ferdinand and his sycophantic courtiers. The Duke makes clear what role he expects his courtiers to play:

Methinks you that are courtiers should be my touchwood, take fire when I give fire; that is, laugh when I laugh, were the subject never so witty.

(I.ii.43–6)

The commentary of Delio and Antonio establishes that the Cardinal and Ferdinand, for all their consciousness of the extent of their influence, will not be a force for good within their court. The Duchess, on the other hand, is a model to be imitated, at least in Antonio's opinion:

> Let all sweet ladies break their flatt'ring glasses,
> And dress themselves in her.

(I.ii.129–30)

It is noticeable that Antonio's metaphor here is a peculiarly feminine one, and the terms in which he praises the Duchess's virtues are limited ones; he singles out her discourse 'full of rapture', her sweet look, her 'sweet countenance' and her divine continence. All these are very much private and female attributes. She is a pattern for 'sweet ladies', as distinct from a general moral exemplar for all subjects, as her brothers ought, but do not attempt, to be.

The three siblings fail, in their different ways, to fulfil their duties as ideal Princes, and for this reason the moral character of the court, as depicted in the commentaries of Bosola and others, as well as more directly, takes on a peculiar quality, and one which is almost antithetical to the humanist conception expressed by Antonio. His speech presents a theoretical concept, the behaviour of the Aragonian brethren a working practice. According to this, the distinction between public and private life is an absolute one.

In public a prince must live up to expectations and play his part: he rules by fear and not by love, and displays of power and caprice are an accepted part of the role. He acts secretly, and by means of agents, and his decisions, even if arbitrary, cannot be questioned. Antonio personifies this Machiavellian conception in his description of Ferdinand:

> What appears in him mirth, is merely outside,
> If he laugh heartily, it is to laugh

> All honesty out of fashion ...
> He speaks with others' tongues, and hears men's suits
> With others' ears; will seem to sleep o'th' bench
> Only to trap offenders in their answers;
> Dooms men to death by information,
> Rewards, by hearsay.

(I.ii.95–102)

In the court of such a Prince, the office of informant or intelligencer is a vital one; but of course such a person cannot be openly appointed, for his whole function depends on secrecy and deception. Hence the Cardinal, although strongly desirous that Bosola be hired as a spy, makes a point of spurning him conspicuously in public. And Bosola in turn plays his part by pretending friendship to the Duchess so convincingly that she reveals the truth of her marriage to him, and thus brings about her own ruin. Ferdinand's publicly mercurial nature – 'a most perverse and turbulent' outside – is useful in confusing observers about his real intentions, and makes life all the more difficult for his followers, who are obliged to adapt their own behaviour to suit his. The courtier's role, too, is reliant on deceptive appearances. Bosola's advice to Castruchio, who wishes to be taken for 'an eminent courtier', stresses the need to observe the forms rather than the substance of wisdom, and to adopt postures of inscrutability:

I would have you learn to twirl the strings of your band with a good grace; and in a set speech, at th' end of every sentence, to hum, three or four times, or blow your nose till it smart again, to recover your memory. When you come to be a president in criminal causes, if you smile upon a prisoner, hang him, but if you frown upon him, and threaten him, let him be sure to 'scape the gallows.

(II.i.6–12)

For their part, the common people and those at the mercy of courtiers' whims have no respect for their superiors and no sense of obligation towards them. Antonio is not surprised that the Duchess's retinue shrinks drastically in her time of misfortune; Bosola expects that dependents should act 'like the mice/That forsake falling houses' (V.ii.204–205). Antonio in his dying breath hopes that his son may 'fly the courts of princes'.

The question of whether the distinction between eminent people and the rest is something absolute or merely an illusion fostered by those to whom it will be of advantage is raised in several ways by the play, though not necessarily given a conclusive answer. Bosola's cynical advice to Castruchio in II.i suggests the latter view, but there is of course a difference between Princes and courtiers. When he is preparing the

Duchess for death in his guise of tomb-maker in IV.ii, he asserts both her part in the common human condition and her exceptional nature. She is human in her frailty, 'a box of worm seed, at best, but a salvatory of green mummy' (IV.ii.124), but she is distinguished by her rank. Bosola's point here, in this dialogue which, as he says, is designed to bring her 'By degrees to mortification', is that to be a Duchess is not an honour but a liability. When she asks, 'Am not I thy Duchess?' his reply is a reminder of the burdens, not the privileges of rank:

Thou art some great woman, sure; for riot begins to sit on thy forehead, (clad in grey hairs) twenty years sooner than on a merry milkmaid's.

(IV.ii.135–6)

Her response to his speech, 'I am Duchess of Malfi still', has been interpreted in many ways, from heroic self-assertion in the face of a meaningless world to the vainglorious defiance of an arrogant aristocrat. Since a play by its nature is capable of yielding meanings according to the particular emphases imparted by its interpreters on the stage, it is not appropriate to pick on a single interpretation as the only right one. Certainly the Duchess's replies to Bosola are spirited and courageous, and for this we are likely to admire them; but at the same time we may also perceive the way in which he is directing the dialogue so as to bring the Duchess to a proper condition of humility before death. He answers her statement of identity with a sentence, used previously in *The White Devil*, denying the reality of eminence :

> That makes thy sleeps so broken:
> *Glories, like glow-worms, afar off shine bright,*
> *But look'd to near, have neither heat or light.*

(IV.ii.142–4)

When eventually the executioners appear with the grisly tools of their trade, the Duchess's manner is one of dignified submission and acceptance. She observes the due order of the last moments of earthly life, wishing well to her brothers (IV.ii.169), considering her legacy to her maidservant (IV.ii.200), and thinking of her children's welfare. In contrast to Cariola she makes no attempt to escape her fate, and behaves with complete self-possession. Her last act is one of resignation, and of recognition that her earthly status has no more significance; all are equal in death.

> Yet stay, heaven gates are not so highly arch'd
> As princes' palaces: they that enter there
> Must go upon their knees.

(IV.ii.232–4)

Death humbles Princes, and ultimately rank ceases to matter, as Delio's final speech, likening the fame of Princes to footprints made in snow emphasizes, yet there does seem to be an implicit recognition in the play that in life Princes and great ones are different from the rest by virtue of their birth. Castruchio can never become a true courtier, however carefully he imitates a courtier's mannerisms; for all her intimacy with the Duchess, Cariola can only die like a servant. Bosola, although without illusions about his masters and their followers, is finally glad to meet his death in their company:

> It may be pain, but no harm to me to die
> In so good a quarrel.

> (V.v.99–100)

It is a commonplace at the end of a revenge tragedy for the revenger to express satisfaction in his association, albeit in death, with those of high rank. Vendice, for instance, at the end of *The Revenger's Tragedy*, is glad to die 'after a nest of dukes'. Bosola feels himself exalted through his involvement in a 'good' quarrel, so that he makes a dignified end, malcontent no longer.

In Bosola's case, his ambition and his desire for identity have never been expressed in terms of a wish for social advancement. In Antonio, however, Webster deals explicitly with the man of middle status who finds himself involved in the lives of great ones. Ironically, Antonio is both the spokesman for order and hierarchy as an ideal, and also the disrupter of these things in his marriage to the Duchess. Webster might have given us a simple perspective on this apparent contradiction by making Antonio a youthful idealist, whose theoretical notions do not stand up to the test of the temptations of sex and ambition, but this does not seem to be the case. Antonio has been 'long in France', and he is recognized by all as an experienced man suitable for employment as the head of the Duchess's household, a role analogous to that played by Malvolio in *Twelfth Night*, but on a far grander scale. The Duchess looks up to him for advice and guidance, and it would clearly be a distortion of the play to see her as an older woman choosing a young man for her pleasure. When he catches the drift of her meaning in the wooing scene he does not hesitate to express his sense of the dangers of his position; the symbolic use of gesture here strongly underlines the meaning of the dialogue. The Duchess, affecting to notice that Antonio has a bloodshot eye, offers him the touch of her ring, drawing attention to the significance of the removal of this ring from her finger:

> 'twas my wedding ring,
> And I did vow never to part with it,
> But to my second husband.
>
> (I.ii.327–9)

Her meaning is implicit, and Antonio at once shows he has caught it, but he hesitates to accept her offer of marriage, realizing how he will appear to the outside world if he does so:

> There is a saucy and ambitious devil
> Is dancing in this circle.
>
> (I.ii.332–3)

The Duchess wittily takes up and extends his metaphor in completing her gesture of putting the ring on his finger, which he kneels to receive, and then proceeds to another symbolic act, raising Antonio up literally to her own level. Her language delicately recognizes and defines their relationship:

> This goodly roof of yours is too low built,
> I cannot stand upright in't, nor discourse,
> Without I raise it higher: raise yourself,
> Or, if you please, my hand to help you: so.
>
> (I.i.336–9)

The business of the ring and the kneeling produces an effect of ceremony; yet in essence this scene is also an anti-ceremony, a ritual of disorder, in which the characters are rejecting or undermining the values of society implicit in a publicly celebrated marriage. Antonio does not refuse the Duchess, but his reply, more openly worded than her offer and perhaps suggestive of a cruder nature, insists on the risks of his own position, and demands reassurances and guarantees:

> Conceive not, I am so stupid, but I aim
> Whereto your favours tend. But he's a fool
> That, being a-cold, would thrust his hands i'th' fire
> To warm them.
>
> (I.ii.345–8)

Antonio then goes with open eyes into the 'wilderness' (I.ii.281) with the Duchess, allowing his scruples to be overcome by feelings, predominantly sexual passion, but not without a leavening of ambition.

Their difference in rank continues to be a theme. It is several times an implicit subject of their dialogue, sometimes in a privately playful way, at others more seriously. For instance when the Duchess tries to make Antonio keep his hat on in her presence, as if they were social equals and the gesture of removing a hat in token of respect had no real significance, he refuses complicity with her; but he does allow himself and her the luxury of a private joke, in the double-entendre of 'I have seen, in colder countries than in France,/Nobles stand bare to th' prince'. (II.i.30–1). In the intimate bedroom scene of III.ii. Antonio again develops a pun from the Duchess's words which plays on the inversions within their relationship. When she calls him, laughingly, a lord of misrule, he answers, 'Indeed, my rule is only in the night,' implying that he is like a lord of misrule not only in being a master of nocturnal sport, but also in having no acknowledged status in the day. That the lord of misrule was often very young or of low rank is also part of Antonio's meaning, if not of his wife's. Later in the scene, after Ferdinand's threats, she devises a stratagem to cover his escape from her house to Ancona in which they act out before Bosola and the officers a little play of mistress dismissing a dishonest servant: again the lines are loaded with extra meanings available to themselves only, as for instance in lines like the Duchess's

> Gentlemen,
> I would have this man be an example to you all:
> So shall you hold my favour
>
> (III.ii.189–90)

or Antonio's

> I am all yours; and 'tis very fit
> All mine should be so.
>
> (III.ii.205–206)

But this situation has its more obviously serious side; the Duchess and Antonio are playing out a desperate game based on their real-life situation, and perhaps in some way Antonio has been a false steward to the Duchess, even if he has not been working so directly against her interests as the character he plays in her fiction.

Antonio, then, far from enjoying any advantages from his rapid if clandestine rise in status, is soon to find that fulfilling ambition in 'the left-hand way' (III.i.29) brings only insecurity and danger. He must involve himself in stratagems and lies to protect his wife's honour, and he must endure the envious sneers of both courtiers and common people. He must bear insult without the right of reply, and although he has initially the satisfactions of domestic life, marriage, parenthood and love, even these things must eventually be sacrificed. When he returns to the play in Act V after a long time offstage he is still not without ambitions or expectations for the future; but in the face of all that has happened during Act IV (although of course Antonio knows nothing of the fates of his wife and children) these ambitions now appear naïve and almost ridiculous. Despite Delio's warnings, Antonio thinks it possible to be reconciled to his brothers-in-law, and perhaps even to bring about a reformation in the Cardinal. He believes that an unexpected midnight appearance in the Cardinal's chamber may startle this cold sinner into remorse:

> It may be that the sudden apprehension
> Of danger (for I'll go in mine own shape)
> When he shall see it fraught with love and duty,
> May draw the poison out of him, and work
> A friendly reconcilement.

> (V.i.67–71)

In these lines the antecedent of 'it' is ambiguous; it might be either the 'sudden apprehension/Of danger' or Antonio's 'own shape'. The latter makes better sense, in which case Antonio comes across as even more naïve, if he believes that his appearance, representing and bearing the marks of love and duty, will move the heart of a man like the Cardinal. The echo scene chastens him and makes him both more resolute and more desperate. He has fought against the belief that his life has no meaning but now he gives in to it, and when he hears, after Bosola's misdirected death-blow, that his wife and children are dead, he dies hopelessly:

> I would not now
> Wish my wounds balm'd, nor heal'd: for I have no use
> To put my life to.

> (V.iv.61–3)

This last simple phrase is extremely poignant for Antonio, the 'complete man' so admired by his wife for his active virtues. His usefulness is at an end, his efforts as a servant of virtue unrewarded. His last wish is that his son may escape the fate of an ambitious court servant like himself.

At the heart of the debate in this play about order and disorder and how a Prince ought to behave stands the Duchess herself. Her deliberate defiance of convention in choosing Antonio for her second husband may seem heroic and admirably courageous, especially in comparison with the style of princely behaviour demonstrated by her brothers. Webster carefully places her act of choice within an established framework in which a whole system of moral values is implied. Antonio's speech defining the ideal order of the French court, followed by Bosola's commentary on the Duke and the Cardinal and the short scenes in which the brothers exemplify a Machiavellian rather than a humanist concept of the Prince, all precede the Duchess's wooing of Antonio and provide the audience with a perspective from which to view it. Despite the views expressed in *Hamlet* about second marriages for widows (which are probably the best-known if not necessarily the most representative Elizabethan views on this subject) the practice was common in England in this period, and was accepted as natural and even advisable, especially for a young widow with children. The attitudes of Ferdinand and the Cardinal are clearly perverse. The former's cryptic words to Bosola –

> she's a young widow,
> I would not have her marry again . . .
> Do not you ask the reason: but be satisfied,
> I say I would not.
>
> (I.ii.179–82)

– immediately invite speculation about the sort of motives which must be cloaked in such secrecy, and the Cardinal's gloomy assertion that 'The marriage night / Is the entrance into some prison' (I.ii.246) suggests the bias of a joyless cleric. In these terms, the Duchess's act of self-assertion speaks out for life and natural instinct against perversion and death:

> Shall this move me? If all my royal kindred
> Lay in my way unto this marriage:
> I'ld make them my low foot-steps.
>
> (I.ii.263–5)

But in committing herself to the secrecy, dissimulation and even shame that marriage to her steward involves, the Duchess is contravening a system of moral and social order that she ought, in terms of the world of the play, to conform to. She has moments of self-questioning expressed, for instance, in her recognition of 'The misery of us, that are born great' and cannot express themselves directly; but in the role-playing games, already discussed, which she devises for herself and Antonio, there is perhaps an attempt to transform reality or relegate it to the realms of fantasy. Neither of them is unaware that their chosen way will create hardships but they are unprepared for the extent of the violence and horror to be unleashed. The Duchess early on realizes that the in-directness necessary to the behaviour of a Prince is equivocal:

117

> We
> Are forc'd to express our violent passions
> In riddles, and in dreams, and leave the path
> Of simple virtue, which was never made
> To seem the thing it is not.

(I.ii.363–7)

But neither she nor Antonio sees that what they have done will be morally destructive. Hounded by Bosola on the night of the baby's birth, and forced to extremities of lying and dissimulation, Antonio recognizes bitterly the validity of a truism:

> *The great are like the base; nay, they are the same,*
> *When they seek shameful ways to avoid shame.*

(II.iii.51–2)

But it is now too late. By choosing the private over the public, the world of love instead of the world of duty, the Duchess has attempted to evade the responsibilities of her rank; she has defied custom and order, and must accordingly suffer exposure, shame and humiliation.

Yet the attitude of the play towards her transgression is not simple or clear-cut. It is and must be recognized as a transgression, and although the court world of Malfi falls far short of the ideal realized outside the play in the court of France, there is no implication that the Duchess's act constitutes an attempt to assert a new kind of order. The collapse of order, on a large scale, is abetted by such an act of individualism. The Duchess does not opt out of her world of status and privilege; 'I am Duchess of Malfi still', she asserts, moments before death. She tries to impose her own desires on an old order, and she is necessarily destroyed in the attempt. Society is reconstituted but only after the deaths of these disorderly Princes; Antonio's son, though his father wished him to fly the courts of Princes, is to be established as his mother's successor. The forms of social order are re-established.

Revenge

Though *The Duchess of Malfi* is not a revenge play in the mould of *The Spanish Tragedy* or *The Revenger's Tragedy*, centring on an individual's vengeance for a personal wrong committed against him or his family, revenge is a significant motif. As Fredson Bowers points out in *Elizabethan Revenge Tragedy*, Webster modifies the usual pattern by having as his protagonist the victim of the villains' revenge, instead of the revenger, by making her die early and by extending the role of the tool-villain to continue the play into its fifth act. The motivating action of the play, the Duchess's marriage, is not in itself a crime, though it might be considered an act of disobedience if the Duchess is thought to subserve her brothers as seems to be the case. The punishment meted out to her by the Cardinal and Ferdinand is a revenge, in the Cardinal's case for the dishonour she has brought to the family name, in Ferdinand's for motives more obscure and personal. The Cardinal never uses the term revenge, perhaps because his attitude to the Duchess's marriage, in no way differentiated from his response to the news of her having given birth, is so straightforwardly that of the aristocrat proud of his royal blood and angry at its tainting. It is not a personal feeling and Webster does not explore it in any detail; it is simply a conventional motive, to illuminate by contrast the peculiar nature of Ferdinand's attitude. Ferdinand several times refers to his revenge ('I account it the honourabl'st revenge,/Where I may kill, to pardon', 'To feed a fire as great as my revenge', 'her innocence and my revenge'), and even expresses the strange idea that his sister's behaviour may constitute an act of divine vengeance against himself and his brother for their sin. It is often taken as accepted doctrine these days that Ferdinand's violent anger against his sister's marriage is caused by his incestuous love for her. The editor of the standard edition of Webster's works, F. L. Lucas, did not agree with this idea, considering it over-ingenious for the original audience; he writes, 'The analysis Ferdinand gives of his own motives at the end of Act IV, though muddled, is clearly intended to be accepted as true. An Elizabethan audience was simple and would certainly have swallowed it' (*The Complete Works of John Webster*, II, 23).

The trouble with this is that Ferdinand's analysis is not only muddled, but ambiguous. The passage referred to is the following:

> I bade thee, when I was distracted of my wits,
> Go kill my dearest friend, and thou hast done't.
> For let me but examine well the cause;
> What was the meanness of her match to me?
> Only I must confess, I had a hope,
> Had she continu'd widow, to have gain'd
> An infinite mass of treasure by her death:
> And that was the main cause; her marriage,
> That drew a stream of gall quite through my heart.

(IV.ii.277–85)

Modern editors punctuate the penultimate line in different ways, sometimes making a very strong break after 'main cause', to imply that the 'infinite mass of treasure' is a false explanation designed to put Bosola off the scent, and that the ruminating phrase which follows ('her marriage, / That drew a stream of gall quite through my heart') is a confession of Ferdinand's true, if unexplained, feeling of bitter resentment. This is the only examination of his motives given to Ferdinand, and one can perhaps deduce more from the abrupt and disjointed form of it than from what the words say. It may be the case as M. C. Bradbrook suggests in *John Webster, Citizen and Dramatist*, that the incest theory is an example of modern revisionism, a 'serviceable' explanation for something ultimately darker, more mysterious, less defined, in Ferdinand's nature. Consuming, but inexplicable, passion is a keynote of his character as Webster presents it, and onstage this violent, almost demonic, intensity may be made convincing without a specific cause assigned. His torture and killing of his sister are acts of revenge, the more terrifying because they show a nature in the grip of violently destructive feelings which it cannot comprehend or control; and his revenge becomes, of course, an act of self-destruction. After the self-inflicted darkness in which he has conducted his last interviews with his sister, the sight of her face in death dazzles his eyes, and the brilliance of her beauty and youth is unbearable. In the agony of guilt he goes mad.

The revenge motif enters a different phase in the last act of the play, and is used, more conventionally, as a way of drawing events together and winding up the play. Bosola, functionally the tool-villain, now assumes another role. It may be that Webster was wiser in being less precise about Ferdinand's motivation, because the rather specific kind of self-explanation he provides for Bosola at this point is hard to reconcile with the nature of the malcontent scholar and cynical commentator exhibited to us earlier. Bosola, confronted by Ferdinand's strange remorse after the murder, presents himself as the servant asking for 'The reward due to my service'; but Ferdinand refuses, insisting that Bosola, 'Get thee into some unknown part o'th' world / That I may never see thee.' Then Bosola, apparently offended, gives an account of his actions in the play which scarcely tallies with what we have seen:

> Let me know
> Wherefore I should be thus neglected? Sir,
> I served your tyranny: and rather strove
> To satisfy yourself, than all the world;
> And though I loath'd the evil, yet I lov'd
> You that did counsel it: and rather sought
> To appear a true servant than an honest man.

(IV.ii.325–31)

This speech considerably simplifies the complex character in which he has appeared up to this point, but seems to function as a preparation for what happens next. Bosola is left alone with the body of the Duchess, who comes briefly to life to utter two words, and then dies. In the last moments of the scene he undergoes a total change of heart; moved by the 'sacred innocence' of the Duchess to an awareness of his own guilty conscience, he weeps over her body, prepares to carry out her last wishes, and then to move into a new phase of life.

In the last act he becomes the Duchess's revenger, making deliberate but ultimately hopeless efforts to save Antonio, formerly his enemy. The attempts, of course, fail and, appropriately, it is Bosola himself who, in the dark, gives Antonio his death-wound. There is a kind of conventional neatness about this device which is not consistent with the more exploratory style of dramaturgy of the major part of the play, and suggests that Webster is less interested in structuring his conclusion in a significant way than in tidying up loose ends. The dying Bosola is asked by courtiers, who include the virtuous Marquis of Pescara, to explain the holocaust around him. His reply is conventionally comprehensive:

> Revenge, for the Duchess of Malfi, murdered
> By th' Aragonian brethren; for Antonio,
> Slain by this hand; for lustful Julia,
> Poison'd by this man; and lastly, for myself,
> That was an actor in the main of all,
> Much 'gainst mine own good nature, yet i'th' end
> Neglected.
>
> (V.v.81–7)

The revised conception of his role formulated at the end of Act IV, as the basically good-hearted servant forced against his will into crime and finally unrewarded appears again. Bosola as revenger, on behalf of the Duchess, Antonio and Julia, as well as himself, is a cardboard figure. He provides that summary view of the action, which is usual at the end of a revenge play, like Horatio's, 'Let me speak to th'yet unknown world / How these things came about. So shall you hear / Of carnal, bloody, and unnatural acts . . .' (V.ii.73–5), at the conclusion of *Hamlet*, though without the accents of joy at the success of the revenge, as expressed, for instance, by Lodovico in *The White Devil*. For Bosola's has been a bungled revenge, 'Such a mistake as I have often seen / In a play', ending in the opposite of what he set out to do. Clearly Webster was experimenting with the formulas of revenge drama in *The Duchess of Malfi*; the vestiges that remain show how far he had moved away from the old conventions, but also the extent to which he was still prepared to draw upon them to bring his play to its conclusion.

Morality

The couplet with which Delio, who seems intended as the wise, objective commentator, concludes the play suggests in conventional terms that there are transcendent and absolute spiritual values which exist beyond the relative values of this world:

> *Integrity of life is fame's best friend,*
> *Which nobly, beyond death, shall crown the end.*

But how far does the play as a whole, in its vision of human life, support such an idea? Concepts like innocence and corruption, suffering, pity and love are clearly essential to Webster's depiction of the lives and deaths of his characters, but it is much harder to define absolutes of good and evil. The physical darkness in which so many scenes take place seems to represent the spiritual darkness of their world, and the blind fumbling in which Bosola kills friend in mistake for enemy suggests how hopeless is any human attempt to act rationally and do good. Evil is not defined in relation to goodness or balanced against opposing forces, but instead is omnipresent.

Certain characters – the Duchess, Antonio, Delio, Pescara – stand apart from the rest, it is true, but with the exception of Pescara, whose role is a very minor one, none of them could be described as unequivocally good or untainted by some of the qualities common to the majority. Delio is venial enough to be attracted to the lascivious Julia, Antonio is both sufficiently ambitious and sufficiently weak to be persuaded to act against his reason, and the Duchess oblivious to all else follows her own desires with an intensity of commitment shared with Ferdinand. Some of the play's sinister images of witchcraft relate to her, and her beauty and sexuality cannot be totally separated from her 'rank blood'.

Several of the characters act in ways they explicitly regard as good, innocent or well-intentioned, but these actions meet with no better outcomes than if they had been deliberately base or evil. The Duchess thinks of her marriage in terms of an emblem of inner peace and harmony against the chaos of the world outside:

> All discord, without this circumference,
> Is only to be pitied, and not fear'd.

(I.ii.387–8)

The imagery of the circle, used by the lovers in reference to their embrace, of the 'sacred Gordian', the mystical knot of marriage, of their affection as planetary spheres, of palm-trees which are only fruitful if planted together, all draw on notions of order and perfection; but of course it is impossible for the marriage to remain as this self-contained, privately harmonious society without any disturbance from the public world, and very soon Antonio and the Duchess find themselves deeply involved in all the dissimulations of public life they had sought to avoid. 'Methinks unjust actions/Should wear these masks and curtains; and not we' (III.ii.157–8), cries the Duchess bitterly, but masks, veils and concealment are as essential for the virtuous as for the vicious in court life. Bosola laments 'That we cannot be suffer'd/To do good when we have a mind to it' when his attempts to revive and console the dying Duchess fail; the impotence of the human will to good is demonstrated even more clearly, of course, in the fiasco of Antonio's death. Antonio's own last-ditch efforts to confront the Cardinal and bring him to remorse misfire disastrously. On the other hand the Cardinal and Ferdinand are only too successful in their projects to destroy their sister's marriage and bring her to humiliation and death. Bosola's machinations succeed also, even though he undertakes them in a spirit of self-loathing:

> O, that to avoid ingratitude
> For the good deed you have done me, I must do
> All the ill man can invent.

(I.ii.197–200)

The ways in which the characters, both good and bad, meet their deaths demonstrate neither any principle of divine retribution nor earthly justice. It is sometimes claimed that the courageous and even spiritually admirable way in which the Duchess confronts her death, and the potent after-effect of her goodness on Bosola help to vindicate the suffering and cruelty of her fate. True, she acts with moving dignity and speaks with fine eloquence in her last moments, and the recognition of her 'sacred innocence' persuades Bosola to attempt to atone for the evils of his life of service to Ferdinand and the Cardinal; yet ultimately Bosola's conversion does no good to anyone else, and all involved die without repentance. In fact repentance is not an option for any of these characters, and illumination of only a very limited kind is demonstrated. The Cardinal is made to perceive the operation of a simple moral principle in the manner of his death:

> O Justice:
> I suffer now for what hath former been:
> *Sorrow is held the eldest child of sin.*

(V.v.52–4)

Does the conventional ring of this sententious couplet imply a triteness and superficiality in this moral judgement? There is justice of a tit-for-tat kind perhaps. Bosola gets 'payment' for his life of service in that he and his master Ferdinand deal one another their death-wounds; he receives the only reward he could now want, and he achieves revenge on 'the main cause of my undoing'. Master and servant are equal at last. Bosola has also the satisfaction of seeing the dwindling of the Cardinal's eminence, not simply in his death alone but in the humiliating exigencies he has been put to, in murdering Julia and concealing her body:

> I do glory
> That thou, which stood'st like a huge pyramid
> Begun upon a large and ample base,
> Shall end in a little point, a kind of nothing.

(V.v.76–9)

The Cardinal's last wish, to be 'laid by, and never thought of' seems to recognize the truth of Bosola's words. Ferdinand dies on a couplet, which again appears to offer illumination into his life:

> My sister. O! my sister, there's the cause on't.
> *Whether we fall by ambition, blood, or lust,*
> *Like diamonds we are cut with our own dust.*

(V.v.71–3)

But again there is no real revelation, for although Ferdinand's words are ambiguous, their possible meanings tell us nothing new. Is he saying that every man is his own worst enemy? Or that what is most closely kin to oneself is the cause of one's downfall? Compared with the state of self-knowledge achieved by Shakespeare's tragic heroes, say Othello or Macbeth, these realizations are minimal indeed.

In *The Duchess of Malfi* Webster is not concerned with transcendence, with showing us how the human spirit can become something greater and finer than its circumstances and rise above the world in which it has its being. The poet Rupert Brooke, who admired Webster's work for the brilliance of its language, described the characters as 'writhing grubs in an immense night'. The sense of moral anarchy in the play is great, perhaps even overwhelming. The Duke and the Cardinal, representatives of secular and of ecclesiastical authority, are evil both personally and in the way they use their power. The court is corrupt, and although its corruption is perceived by Antonio and Delio they cannot take any actions which will purify it. The play's ending does not suggest the fulfilment of a moral process by which a decadent regime is overthrown, as in *Macbeth*, or a tainted dynasty brought down, as in *Hamlet*, and replaced by a new and uncorrupted order. Antonio's son has survived alone of his family, and in spite of an unfavourable horoscope, but his unspeaking presence in the play's last moments is a mere token, a nod to the conventions of ending a tragedy on a note of quiet, by no means an affirmation of a new order established.

Yet there are reasons for us to take seriously what Webster has to say of human life, and the play has qualities beyond simply 'poetic power', which does not exist in the abstract, especially not in a piece written for theatrical presentation. His depiction of a mysterious, irrational world in which the wills of those in power, emancipated from all normal considerations of ethics and morality, reign supreme, is intensely convincing. Good and evil are irrelevant in those supreme moments of horror or agony when the human spirit is put to the test, when for example the Duchess is able to invite her executioners to end her life, first kneeling before them, or in Webster's vision of the horrific unknowableness of existence, as when Bosola enters, to an empty darkened stage, having just heard word of his own death from the lips of the Cardinal, footsteps sound, and the mad Ferdinand comes on musing to himself, 'Strangling is a very quiet death.' 'Blind' is a word often used of the struggles of Webster's characters, and the idea of total moral and spiritual impercipience is implied in Brooke's quotation; yet there is also a brilliance, a lucidity, momentary and transforming as a flash of lightning, at the high point of this play which makes us perceive our own greyer world differently, even if it is not illuminated by Webster's.

6. Stagecraft

The stagecraft of *The Duchess of Malfi* is in some ways more experimental than that of *The White Devil* and still further from the regular conventions of the revenge genre. This is not to say that it makes little use of artifice or theatrical devices, which is far from true, but the elements of staging which give the play its generally non-realistic and overtly 'theatrical' character are fully integrated into the play's overall style and form an essential part of its meaning.

The title-page of the play states that it was 'Presented privately, at the Blackfriers; and publiquely at the Globe'. The two theatres were rather different in nature, the former smaller in size, indoor, and artificially lighted, the latter a public theatre with cheaper prices, capable of holding nearly twice as many people, and outdoors, so that performances utilized natural light. It was not at all unusual for plays of this period to be presented on both public and private stages, and many of Shakespeare's Globe theatre plays, such as *Macbeth* and *Othello*, were also performed, in different conditions, at the Blackfriars or at court. Although the wording of *The Duchess of Malfi*'s title-page need not be significant in this respect, there are indications that the play may have been written with presentation at the Blackfriars theatre in mind. The breaks between each act (in contrast to the continuous movement of *The White Devil*) not only seem designed to allow for the inter-act music that was customary in the private theatres, as demonstrated, for instance, in *The Knight of the Burning Pestle*, but also make more sense of the play if they are strongly marked; in particular, the time-gap between Acts II and III requires to be represented by some break in the continuity of the performance if the remarks of Antonio and Delio at the beginning of III.i on the passage of time are not to seem ludicrous. The large number of intimate scenes between two or three characters, where the situation is private or domestic, the tone quiet and the style of action almost realistic, suggests a small-scale presentation where subtleties of mood and expression would be significant; the scene in which the Duchess woos Antonio, for instance, or the first part of III.ii where the Duchess prepares for bed, must be played delicately. Large-scale, grand effects would be out of place here. Indications of setting are often provided in this play, and significant distinctions made between public and private, interior and exterior, light and dark. The alteration between these polarities is important in thematic terms. It is necessary to state at the outset that not all experts on the Elizabethan and Jacobean stage are agreed on the extent to which staging in public and private theatres differed, particularly with regard to ways in which the indoor, private theatres could increase or diminish light onstage by bringing on or removing candles and torches. Some critics also feel that the famous night-time scenes in Elizabethan and Jacobean drama, for instance the scene in the Capulets' tomb in *Romeo and Juliet* or *Othello* V.i., were actually designed to be played so that every action was clearly visible and the darkness symbolic rather than illusionistic. Public theatre plays of course contain many scenes set at night or in the dark, and internalized stage directions in the dialogue (like the well-known line of Horatio from *Hamlet*, 'look, the morn in russet mantle clad . . .') provide information about time and setting which did not have to be represented in any way. Nonetheless, it may also be felt that in a play like *The Duchess of Malfi*, where the relation of physical to moral or spiritual darkness is so important, the use of visual effects to provide light/dark contrasts, and the capacity of the stage to be at least partially darkened for some moments would be important considerations.

For instance, in Act II, significant changes of setting and lighting are indicated several times, and some way of actualizing these would undoubtedly assist in making the dramatist's point. The first scene, like the opening of the play, is a formal scene set in a royal presence-chamber, where courtiers attend on the Prince to present suits or offer gifts, and the Prince is publicly on display. Characters enter in ones and twos, Bosola and Castruchio, the Old Lady, Antonio and Delio, 'talking apart', of their own private concerns, and waiting, before the Prince, or in this case the Duchess, enters with attendants to give the scene its focus and purpose. The formality, however, breaks down in disorder, when Bosola's gift of apricots precipitates the Duchess's labour, and she leaves in desperate haste. The lights that are called for by the Duchess and Delio to help her to her chamber imply departure down the dark corridors of a Renaissance palace. This large-scale public scene involving many characters and moving from disparate group conversations between pairs of characters to a single situation which provides a focus for everyone present gives place to a shorter, less formal, unlocalized scene, the main purpose of which is to represent the disorder brought about in the household by the Duchess's labour and the need to conceal it. Time is indicated – 'This evening', 'till the sun-rising'; the mood is one of tension. Then comes II.iii, the first scene which is obviously meant to take place both in the dark and in an outside setting. Bosola, the spy lurking about for 'intelligence', enters with a lantern. The atmosphere is sinister and frightening; there are strange noises, which might be the rising of the wind or the screaming of a solitary owl. Antonio, when he comes in, cannot at first make out Bosola in the dark, and Bosola with his lantern has the advantage:

> Antonio! Put not your face nor body
> To such a forc'd expression of fear,
> I am Bosola; your friend.

> (II.iii.11–13)

The staccato opening exchange between the two men conveys nervousness and anxiety. Antonio sweats despite the coldness of the night air, as Bosola disturbingly remarks; the figure with the light is no friend. Fumbling in the dark, Antonio drops the paper with the child's horoscope, which Bosola, again with the help of his lantern, is able to retrieve.

Plots and stratagems flourish by night. The next scene, in the Cardinal's lodging in Rome, again provides a contrast; Julia, great lady of pleasure, the Cardinal's plaything, belongs indoors, in the kind of luxurious world conjured up by references to falcons and lutes, cassia, civet and gold. Although lust and adultery are the subjects of the scene, the emotional tone is perfectly cool.

In II.iii the effect of darkness is a natural one, in that the scene takes place outdoors at night, although of course the darkness is also symbolic. In IV.i the effect is, if anything, more terrifying, because the darkness is artificial. Ferdinand has vowed (III.ii.141) never to see his sister again, yet he cannot keep away from her presence; Bosola's mediation between them is not satisfactory to him, and he longs, in a strange spirit of self-torture, to discover for himself how she is bearing her imprisonment. Bosola announces the Duke's entry:

> Your elder brother the lord Ferdinand,
> Is come to visit you: and sends you word
> 'Cause once he rashly made a solemn vow
> Never to see you more; he comes i'th' night;
> And prays you, gently, neither torch nor taper
> Shine in your chamber.

> (IV.i.21–6)

Bosola then removes the lights and a short dialogue, in as a complete a darkness as the theatre can afford, follows. For Ferdinand this unnatural situation is the appropriate one for his sister:

> It had been well,
> Could you have liv'd thus always: for indeed
> You were too much i'th' light.

> (IV.i.40–2)

These apparently simple words are loaded with meaning; the Duchess has lived 'too much i'th' light' because too many people have seen her, but also because her behaviour has been 'light', in another sense, at least to Ferdinand. They convey the terrifying quality of Ferdinand's possessiveness and his madness. When he gives her the dead man's hand the revelation should be a shock mainly to her but also to the audience; 'Let her have lights enough,' orders Ferdinand harshly, and no sooner does the Duchess confront one horror than another is produced. The traverse, or discovery-space, is uncovered to reveal the tableau of corpses. The effect should be sudden and violent; lighting changes must be necessary. But of course even when light is restored, there can be no return to the natural world. What the Duchess sees now is not real, though she is in no position to detect the illusion. The ghastly waxen images remain visible for the rest of the scene, and Ferdinand's matter-of-fact explanation of the spectacle to Bosola ('presentations ... but fram'd in wax') goes no way towards restoring normality. The scene which follows, though no special lighting effects are called for, is again a scene of confinement; the Duchess is in a prison, perhaps a dungeon, and the only evidence of a world elsewhere is the dismal howl of madmen.

Physical darkness seems to be a crucial part of the stage spectacle in V.iv. As when Bosola and Antonio met before in II.iii, this is a stormy, night scene. References in the dialogue create atmosphere, and suggest sound effects as of a tempest more than natural:

GRISOLAN: 'Twas a foul storm tonight.
RODRIGO: The Lord Ferdinand's chamber shook like an osier.
MALATESTE: 'Twas nothing but pure kindness in the devil,
To rock his own child.

(V.iv.18–20)

The speeches are short, the language staccato. There is tension and fear in the darkness. Bosola overhears the Cardinal planning his death, but the Cardinal has already disappeared. Ferdinand slips in and out in a moment, murmuring to himself of secret murder, unnoticed by Bosola. Each is lost in his own thoughts and the darkness accentuates the image of spiritual isolation. Antonio enters, also intent on his own purpose of surprising the Cardinal. Bosola hears, but does not identify him, and in the brief moment while a servant is dispatched to get a lantern, deals Antonio his death-blow. The light is brought, but the fatal mistake has been made. That the manner of this killing may seem like a contrivance is recognized in Bosola's description of it as 'Such a mistake as I have often seen / In a play', yet the circumstances of mistaking a friend for a foe in the darkness and achieving the exact opposite of one's true intention are entirely appropriate to the themes and symbolism of this play, where good intentions are all too soon thwarted in an anarchic and unfathomable universe.

Dark and light, then, are used in several ways, both naturalistically, to represent times of day and interior or exterior action, symbolically, to relate to the play's moral themes, and also expressionistically, as a means of denoting outwardly a certain kind or quality of inner experience. Some of the stage properties share this variety of functions, in particular weapons and bodies. It is to be expected that in a play of this kind, where many characters suffer violent deaths, that weapons will be a major property. Yet a number of these weapons are not used to kill, and are produced for purposes other than killing. The first of these is the poniard produced by Ferdinand in I.ii at the end of the long dialogue between the two brothers and the sister on the subject of her remarriage. After the Cardinal has made his exit, leaving the twin brother and sister alone together, Ferdinand unexpectedly draws this small weapon:

> You are my sister,
> This was my father's poniard: do you see,
> I'ld be loath to see't look rusty, 'cause 'twas his.

> (I.ii.252–4)

There would be a sinister fitness in Ferdinand's preserving the steely shine of this inherited poniard by using it on his sister; the weapon seems to represent the family honour, which Ferdinand believes may require his sister's life for its preservation. At the same time there may also be an implied phallicism in the production of the weapon, at this point, as Ferdinand's obscene reference a few lines later, 'that part, which . . ./Hath nev'r a bone in't', might reinforce. It must be the same poniard that Ferdinand brings in III.ii when he surprises his sister by a secret entry into her private chamber, for again his theme is the preservation of her virtue:

> Die, then, quickly.
> Virtue, where art thou hid? What hideous thing
> Is it, that doth eclipse thee?

> (III.ii.71–3)

The dagger is a threat and a symbol, but it is not a weapon of actual violence. It is a kind of sinister gift from brother to sister, foreshadowing the actual death that will be his presentation to her at the end of the masque scene. When Antonio enters at this point, after Ferdinand's sudden exit, he is armed, according to the original stage-direction, with a pistol. Yet his weapon also is not put to the test, and may even suggest by contrast his impotence, at least against those enemies at whom it should be directed. He comes on the scene too late to confront Ferdinand, though all the time he has been concealed behind the arras with Cariola and has witnessed the whole interview; he now wishes that Ferdinand would reappear, not to kill him, but

> That, standing on my guard, I might relate
> My warrantable love.

> (III.ii. 148–9)

There seems to be something at best naïve or inadequate in such a response; clearly Ferdinand in his present state of mind would not be moved by such a relation, and it denotes weakness in Antonio to think so. The other appearance of a pistol in the play has different connotations, but again the pistol functions as a weapon only symbolically. In V.ii Julia surprises Bosola alone with a sudden entry, 'pointing a pistol at him'. He soon disarms her, and it may be the case that, as he supposes, it is a mere toy anyway, but initially he is taken in. For the audience there is a brief moment of shock, for Julia has been seen as a self-willed and unscrupulous woman who acts without principle, and then, perhaps, a laugh and a release of tension when Julia orders her captive to 'confess';

> Yes, confess to me
> Which of my women 'twas you hir'd, to put
> Love-powder into my drink?

(V.ii.152–4)

The pistol here symbolically links sex and death and may perhaps imply a comment on the impotence of woman when she tries to take over the attributes of a man. Julia herself is shortly to be dispatched by an efficient but far less obvious weapon, a poisoned book. Presumably this would be a Bible, so that once again the weapon has significance beyond itself, in the irony that its user is a priest.

The instrument of death that does dispatch the Duchess is the executioners' cords. These are formally offered to her by Bosola as part of the parody marriage-masque in IV.ii at a stage in the proceedings when the royal personage honoured by the masque would be given a presentation.

> Here is a present from your princely brothers,
> And may it arrive welcome, for it brings
> Last benefit, last sorrow.

(IV.ii.165–7)

He adds, 'This is your last presence chamber,' suggesting the formality of the occasion as well as its finality. Like the poisoned book, the cords have their symbolic significance. In terms of their function in the masque, they represent a wedding ring, but also of course the more sinister 'true-love knot'; when Brachiano in *The White Devil* meets death by strangulation, Lodovico ironically offers him 'a true-love knot / Sent from the Duke of Florence'; and when Cariola desperately tries to stave off the moment of death by claiming she is engaged to be married, the executioner answers her, 'Here's your wedding-ring.' The ring has functioned as an ambiguous symbol earlier in the play, in the wooing scene, when the Duchess gives the wedding ring of her first marriage to Antonio, for it is also associated with magic and witchcraft:

> There is a saucy and ambitious devil
> Is dancing in this circle.

(I.ii.332–3)

says Antonio, and displaces the devil with 'small conjuration' by putting the ring on his finger. Shortly before the Duchess is killed, Bosola, now acting as the bellman who makes a speech to condemned prisoners outside their dungeon on the night before execution, and then tolls them on their way to the scaffold, intones a dirge, preparing the Duchess for death. She is urged to

> *Strew your hair with powders sweet:*
> *Don clean linen, bathe your feet,*
> *And, the foul fiend more to check,*
> *A crucifix let bless your neck.*

(IV.ii.18–92)

These are ritual actions of preparation for a Christian death; the implications of diabolism associated with the ring earlier are now explicitly banished.

Webster envisages death by strangulation as non-disfiguring – but quick, though he also thought it possible for the Duchess to revive briefly (as Desdemona does, after being smothered), a few moments later. Her corpse, which is onstage and at the centre of attention for 150 lines, retains its beauty, which is one of the reasons why Ferdinand cannot bear to see her face. There are no wounds or blood. Corpses and effigies are another important stage property in the play, and though there are so many 'strange images of death' (*Macbeth* I.iii.96) there is a curious bloodlessness about most of them. The severed hand that Ferdinand leaves with the Duchess in VI.i is cold but not bloody; the waxen figures of Antonio and his children revealed to her in the same scene form a 'sad spectacle' or theatrical tableau, but the horror of them is cold and frozen, not violent or gory. The use of physical mutilation in *Titus Andronicus*, for instance, provides a strong contrast. Later the strangled corpses of the Duchess's two children, killed offstage, are actually brought on by Bosola for display, or perhaps 'discovered' behind the traverse in an attempt to arouse Ferdinand's pity. Again, these are stage images and do not function in their context to move the emotions of either the onstage characters or the audience. Elsewhere, bodies have a more distinctively physical reality. The Duchess's corpse may be an object for contemplation, but the dead body of Julia is an object which has to be lugged about and disposed of. The disposal in fact presents a problem for the Cardinal, since she has died in his rooms and he needs to ensure that the body is discovered in her own apartment. So he arranges for Bosola to come at midnight to move the body from one place to another. Bosola, who has taken on a number of ghastly duties in the course of the play, answers wryly 'I think I shall/Shortly grow the common bier for churchyards' (V.ii.308–309). Webster then contrives an ingenious use of corpses, for when Bosola turns up to keep his midnight appointment he brings with him another corpse for whose death the Cardinal is also responsible, that of Antonio. If one is to imagine Julia's body still onstage at this point, as logically it would be since she has died in the Cardinal's apartments and he is waiting for Bosola to remove her, it seems as if Webster has quite deliberately filled his stage with corpses for the dénouement of the play. The Cardinal, Ferdinand and finally Bosola himself complete the picture. Again there is an expressionistic quality in this stagecraft which so insistently underlies the ubiquity and inescapability of death; it is present not only in the waxen images, but also in the fatal fumbling in the dark, the long, drawn-out torture of the Duchess, the corpses carried in and carried out, and in the figure of the avenger with his sword: 'Now? Art thou come?' (V.v.7).

In this play Webster draws on a number of devices tried out earlier in *The White Devil* for structuring scenes and passages of dialogue. The use of various kinds of framing devices is carried further. Commentary, by one character or a set of characters, on the actions of others who are onstage at the time, is introduced at the very beginning, appropriately creating the impression that court life is like a series of theatrical scenes played out in front of an audience. Antonio describes to Delio the various 'great courtiers' who enter in groups to fill the presence-chamber like a master of ceremonies: 'Here comes Bosola/The only court-gall . . .' 'Here's the Cardinal,' 'Here comes the great Calabrian Duke,' while Delio plies him with suitable questions: 'What's that Cardinal? I mean his temper?' 'What's his brother?' Bosola plays out a scene with the Cardinal and Ferdinand one with his sycophants, while Antonio and Delio stand to the side and interpret. In III.iii, another public scene, Webster uses the commentary technique less obtrusively but again to make a skilful point about the relation of Princes to their public. The opening stage direction suggests distinctive groupings of the characters: 'Enter Cardinal with Malateste, Ferdinand with Delio and Silvio, and Pescara'. Accordingly, the Cardinal and Count Malateste begin a private dialogue, and Ferdinand another with his two companions a few lines

133

later, commenting on the absurdity of Malateste's military posturing. Pescara, who is separated from the others in the stage direction, and who is, in any case, one of the play's few objectively and one-sidedly 'good' characters, is not involved in either dialogue, and does not speak until the entry of Bosola. Bosola's arrival with an urgent message for the Duke and the Cardinal (in fact, to inform them that the Duchess is married to Antonio) is interestingly treated; since the audience already knows this information there is no need for Bosola to give it again, and Webster concentrates instead on depicting the brothers' reactions, as perceived by Pescara, Delio and company, who now become fascinated spectators of a brief but violently emotional scene:

PESCARA: Mark Prince Ferdinand,
  A very salamander lives in's eye,
  To mock the eager violence of fire.
SILVIO: That cardinal hath made more bad faces with his oppression than
  ever Michael Angelo made good ones: he lifts up's nose, like a foul porpoise
  before a storm –
PESCARA: The Lord Ferdinand laughs.
DELIO: Like a deadly cannon, That lightens ere it
                                                                                          smokes.
                                                                               (III.iii.47–54)

The Princes have only the briefest dialogue together, and Bosola but a single line in the whole scene, but by these economical means Webster conveys much, not only of the relation in which courtiers stand to their Princes, but also of the way that immense conflagrations break out from small beginnings.

Another device for framing a scene, sometimes allowing the audience two perspectives on the action, is the use of overhearing. In I.ii the Duchess deliberately places Cariola behind the arras to act as witness to the private marriage ceremony between herself and Antonio, although, in fact, the marriage would have been completely legal without Cariola's presence. In this instance the fact that, as the audience knows, Cariola is behind the arras throughout the wooing does not modify the impact of the scene to any great extent; but the real significance only emerges later, when Webster repeats the device in III.ii to very different effect. The first scene is undoubtedly intended to be recalled because of the similarity of setting; again it is an intimate scene in the Duchess's private apartment, between the Duchess and Antonio as lovers preparing to sleep together. Cariola is part of their intimacy as before, and her presence serves perhaps to make the scene more domestic, less sensual. Antonio proposes to Cariola to repeat a familiar trick on his wife by stealing unnoticed from the room and leaving the Duchess to talk to herself. Webster marvellously uses the homely marital joke ('I have divers times/Serv'd her the like, when she hath chaf'd extremely') as a prelude to a shock effect; while the Duchess continues to address Antonio as if he were still present, his place is taken by another figure who enters noiselessly from behind: her brother Ferdinand. She turns suddenly and notices him. Harmless teasing modulates in a moment to horror. After a brief but chilling dialogue Ferdinand leaves as suddenly as he came, on the sinister line, 'I will never see you more,' a cross between threat and promise. His absence is at once supplied by the return of Antonio and Cariola, who have all the time been behind the arras. The relation of this scene to the other is an ironic inversion; again the Duchess talks of a second marriage in the presence of an unseen witness, and her first marriage is recalled, but this time this witness is himself the subject of the dialogue, and the Duchess does not know that he is overhearing it. Why does Antonio not enter earlier and confront Ferdinand, especially since Ferdinand gives voice to the suspicion that the Duchess's husband is near at hand? Is it a dramatic convenience, to allow Ferdinand the confrontation, uninterrupted? Or does Antonio's failure to intervene imply a failure of courage?

In the third scene of overhearing, V.v, the failure of intervention is again of crucial importance, though very differently handled. The Cardinal, wishing to keep the coast clear so that he can dispose of Julia's body undisturbed, tells his followers not to enter his apartment whatever strange sounds they may hear, because this will only worsen Ferdinand's condition. This provides neatly for a situation whereby the Cardinal's genuine cries for help as he is threatened by Bosola are overheard by his followers, who are present 'above', but treated as pretence. Because the Cardinal is so cold and evil a character, the scope for black humour is given full rein:

CARDINAL: Here's a plot upon me; I am assaulted. I am lost,
　　　　　Unless some rescue!
GRISOLAN: 　　　　　　　　　He doth this pretty well:
　　　　　But it will not serve to laugh me out of mine honour.
CARDINAL: The sword's at my throat!
RODRIGO: 　　　　　　　　　You would not bawl so loud then.
　　　　　　　　　　　　　　　　　　　(V.v.23–6)

Eventually Pescara, perceiving that 'The accent of the voice sounds not in jest' decides to intervene, but by the time he arrives it is too late, and the courtiers arrive on the scene in the last moments of the play to witness first of all Bosola's statement of responsibility, and then the deaths of the Cardinal and himself.

The play contains less in the way of spectacular effects than *The White Devil*. The last act death scenes take place in an atmosphere of fumbling and mistaken intentions, rather than the splendid theatricality with which Flamineo and Vittoria meet their ends. There are no ghosts, and only one dumbshow, the scene in which the Cardinal is installed as a soldier and the Duchess and Antonio ritually banished from the state of Ancona. The influence of the supernatural is strongly suggested at several points, but much more subtly and less obtrusively than in the earlier play. In the eerie scene (II.iii) where Bosola and Antonio meet in the dark and Antonio drops the horoscope of his newborn son, an atmosphere of ill-fortune is created by the setting, the darkness, and sound effects of wind and unidentified screaming, so that Antonio's nose-bleed, which he discounts as coincidence, seems at once like an omen of evil, particularly since the child (who we do not know at this stage will actually survive) is given a malevolent horoscope. Imagery of witchcraft, diabolism and imminent storms intensifies this atmosphere; the Duchess despite her scorn for superstition has a prophetic dream:

> Methought I wore my coronet of state,
> And on a sudden all the diamonds
> Were chang'd to pearls.

(III.v.13–15)

In the latter part of the play the after-life of the Duchess has a quality of the supernatural, both in IV.ii when her brief return to consciousness after strangulation confirms Bosola in his penitence, in V.ii when for a moment Bosola imagines he can see her, and in the more contrived echo scene (V.iii). Scenes of this kind had been written for previous plays, including Dekker's *Old Fortunatus* and Jonson's *Cynthia's Revels*, but Webster's is a careful adaptation of a device more usual in comedy to replace the ghost who appears in tragedy as a portent of death. The echo comes '*from the Duchess' grave*', according to the stage-direction, and it may be that a representation of the grave would have been present onstage, particularly as at one point Antonio imagines not only that he hears his dead wife's voice but that he also sees her:

ECHO: *Never see her more.*
ANTONIO: I mark'd not one repetition of the Echo
But that: and on a sudden, a clear light
Presented me a face folded in sorrow.

(V.iii.41–4)

White Devil and *The Duchess of Malfi*:
at women of pleasure'

en been noticed that in *The Duchess of Malfi* Webster echoes
tragedy in several ways: there are verbal similarities, even the
complete sententious couplet (*The White Devil* V.i.41–2, *The
Malfi* IV.ii.143–4), repetitions of devices of structure or
such as the deployment of commentator figures and asides,
various kinds of stage-spectacle such as dumbshows, proces-
ublic ceremonies, and the concluding of the play with the
of a member of the new generation. These and other such
dealt with more fully in the separate sections on the two
are also parallels between the characters: Flamineo and
e most obvious pair, but the two Cardinals share similar-
hough less obviously, Francisco and Ferdinand, Zanche

oines are material for contrast rather than comparison;
ifferent way Webster treated the Duchess is the major
fference in tone and tragic effect between the two plays.
cases it is their marriages, taking place at the beginning
ich are principal factors (though not the only ones) in
motion, their functions in the plotting of their plays
imilar. Vittoria appears only in five scenes (I.ii, III.ii,
always at high points of the action, and her part in-
nce towards the end; her surprisingly long absence
roughout the second act shows the extent to which
irected by other characters. On the other hand her
latest possible minute and she is alive to within fifty
play which seems to alternate long and short scenes,
otracted, not just by its length but by the nature of
to several component parts, and in a breathtaking
death is played out to the full before the three real
obviously designed as a grand climax of sensation
which has already demonstrated these qualities in
Duchess has nine scenes (I.i, ii, II.i, III.i, ii, iv, v,
ourse, only through the first four acts; during her
he stage, for four comparatively short scenes in

The echo's hints and cryptic phrases warn Antonio of impending death;
there is also an implication that the Duchess lives on in spirit and watches
over him. The illusoriness of the distinction between life and death is
superbly suggested both by the form of the scene and its setting. In the
last part of the play Webster evokes a sense of swift-moving and in-
exorable fate; Ferdinand's fearsome madness is retributive, and both
Julia and the Cardinal recognize a principle of justice at work in the
manner of their deaths. Bosola hovers like an avenging angel with his
sword, appearing at midnight in the Cardinal's chamber at the very
moment when the latter is recalling a guilty vision:

> When I look into the fishponds in my garden,
> Methinks I see a thing, arm'd with a rake
> That seems to strike at me.
> (*Enter* BOSOLA *and* SERVANT *with* ANTONIO's *body*.)
> Now? Art thou come?

Yet overall Webster does not stress inescapable fate so much as the
darkness and uncertainty of life. In his universe there is no coherent
principle, whether for good or ill, at work; the only possible philosophical
stance is one of sceptical stoicism.

The devices of revenge tragedy such as ghosts, feigned madness,
disguise, dumbshows, are much less in evidence here than in *The White
Devil*, and where they do appear have functions other than merely
moving the plot forward. Ferdinand's madness, for instance, which is
perhaps an extension of his capriciousness and pleasure in feigning, his
'perverse and turbulent nature', as Antonio puts it (I.ii.94), is not essential for the play's dénouement. The only disguise in the play is Bosola's
in IV.ii, as an old man who claims to be a tomb-maker and then a bellman; the function of this is both psychological and symbolic, in that the
Duchess's isolation is intensified by this last, long interview with someone
who knows her but whom she cannot recognize, and Bosola's chosen
roles present her and the audience with a depersonalized image of time
and death. Presumably Bosola removes some part of his disguise when
Ferdinand appears, after the murder of Cariola, but there is no stage
direction for it, and no clear transition for the actor from the disguise
back to the real Bosola. The one dumbshow of the play in III.iv arises
naturally out of Webster's wish to represent a ceremonial action which
could not easily have been presented more directly. It is not essential to
the plot and could have been reported rather than shown; but this way
both the solemnity and the element of shock are increased. The two

commenting pilgrims at the shrine of Our Lady of Loretto 'expect / A noble ceremony' in which the Cardinal will exchange his religious habit for that of a soldier, and the Duchess will 'pay her vow of pilgrimage'; they see the first part of this ceremony, but the latter half takes an unexpected turn when the Duchess and Antonio, having made their vows, are formally and, it seems from the pilgrim's remarks, with some violence, banished. The sight of this wordless ritual, accompanied by 'very solemn music' and choral singing, helps to stress the power of Church and state against which the Duchess and her husband are impotent, but also the way in which the Cardinal can wrench the law of the state to suit his own desires:

SECOND PILGRIM: ... the Pope, forehearing of her looseness,
        Hath seiz'd into th' protection of the Church
        The Dukedom which she held as dowager.
FIRST PILGRIM: But by what justice?
SECOND PILGRIM: Sure, I think by none,
        Only her brother's instigation.

(III.iv.30–4)

The stagecraft of the play is self-conscious, and there is, as has been said, considerable use of role-playing and ritual, and a number of references, particularly by Bosola and the Duchess, to the idea that they see themselves as actors, performing in a 'tedious theatre'. The devices of speech which in *The White Devil* stand out to a modern audience as overtly theatrical (though of course commonplace in the drama of this period), the aside and the sententious couplet, are also less marked in this play. Asides are used from time to time when a character has to provide the audience with information not to be conveyed to the others present, or when a different perspective on the action is to be offered; Bosola, in II.i, testing his suspicion that the Duchess is pregnant with an offering of apricots, draws attention to her reaction in asides: 'Good, her colour rises,' 'How greedily she eats them.' Antonio, confronted by Bosola in the dark and obliged to put on a feigned performance, uses asides to express his real emotions: 'This mole does undermine me,' 'This fellow will undo me.' Such uses are different from Flamineo's in *The White Devil* and much more conventional. Similarly, sententiae are less frequently employed, and not with the same effects of irony and discrepancy. Antonio has most of those which are not exit lines, and they characterize him as a man searching for meanings in life. As one of the speakers who assert normative moral judgements (the other being Delio), he is given several couplets such as:

Some curs'd example poison't [the court]
Death and diseases through the whole lan

The great are like the base; nay, they a
When they seek shameful ways to avo

From decay'd fortunes every flatter
Men cease to build where the foun

Unlike his counterpart Flamineo, Bos
otherwise, and his major meditations
this outward form of man / To be bel
box of worm seed, at best, but a salv
5) – are conspicuously without them
mostly cryptic and fragmented, 'se
couplet, but here the content is
generally applicable. Though the
the sententious couplet is not th

The great effects of *The Duch*
of *The White Devil*, but they sh
transitions between moods an
on the emotions and sensib
lucinatory world of darknes
the boundaries between th
life and death, are consta
the dark where Antonio
ludicrous but also horrif
responses and aims to
of the play's poetry
imagination.

Act II, she is in fact the subject of three of the scenes. Her death scene too is long and protracted, but it cannot be a climax in the same sense as Vittoria's since another act of the play is to follow. She does, however, hold the stage almost continuously for a very long period, and the focus of all Act IV is on her and her suffering; no other character rivals her for attention, as Flamineo does Vittoria up to the actual moment of their deaths. And in the last act of the play, though she is not physically present, her influence on the course of the action is a major theme and symbolically represented in the echo scene where one might assume her voice would be used for the echo. Her role is in all senses a larger one than Vittoria's; and the fact that the title of *The White Devil* refers not only to the play's female protagonist but also to a more general complex of ideas about the deceptiveness of evil also implies that Vittoria functions differently within the play.

The Duchess is more of a focus of interest than Vittoria partly because of her sexual isolation. Her maid Cariola has a distinctly subordinate part; she never appears without the Duchess, and her main function is to illuminate and define the Duchess's role; in the only moment when she holds the centre of the stage, for fifteen lines of undignified dying, her struggles and desperate prevarication with the executioners only serve to throw light on the Duchess's dignity. Julia operates in a sub-plot which never directly impinges on the Duchess at all, and the two women know nothing of one another's lives until Julia learns, a few moments before her own death, that the secret nurtured by her lover the Cardinal is his complicity in the murder of the Duchess. Julia's role is to echo and comment indirectly on the Duchess by her activities as a 'great woman of pleasure'; she has no importance in her own right. In *The White Devil*, though Zanche functions much like Cariola, Isabella and Cornelia are given significance independent of their relation to Vittoria. For one thing, they are her moral opposites, virtuous women who are shown to act from motives other than self-interest. Isabella has only one scene but it establishes her as a forceful presence; there is a strange contrast which impresses itself on the memory between the apparent self-abnegation of her device to cover for Brachiano's infidelity in the presence of her brother, putting herself publicly in the wrong in the interests of preserving family unity, and the vehemence with which she plays her part as jealous wife, fantasizing a violent revenge on her rival:

> To dig the strumpet's eyes out, let her lie
> Some twenty months a-dying, to cut off
> Her nose and lips, pull out her rotten teeth,

141

> Preserve her flesh like mummia, for trophies
> Of my just anger.

(II.i.245–9)

Though she fades from the action early on, her influence lingers, inspiring both her brother and her potential lover (Lodovico) to revenge. Cornelia's role is more attenuated and varied. As mother to Vittoria, Flamineo and Marcello, and widow to a husband who had, according to Flamineo (I.ii.317), been a spendthrift, she is given a social context which helps account for the careers and attitudes of her children. Her lurking presence in I.ii suggests the idea of an outsider who has no part in the extravagance of court life and whose only role at court is to criticize. Like Queen Margaret in *Richard III*, who also hovers unseen upstage and enters the action in order to curse and prophesy doom, she has something supernatural about her, the quality of a voice of doom, and there is horror in the virulence of her curse on her daughter:

> Be thy act Judas-like, betray in kissing;
> May'st thou be envied during his short breath,
> And pitied like a wretch after his death.

(I.ii.266–8)

At the same time, through Cornelia's reactions, the outrageous quality of Vittoria's behaviour is highlighted; not only does she flaunt society's norms in her liaison with a married man, splitting apart a family and helping to bring about a murder, but she also disobeys her parent and disrupts her own family. In Act V Webster draws strongly on Cornelia's role as mother for effects of pathos. She is first obliged to witness one of her sons kill his brother, and then to lie on the murderer's behalf. The loss of Marcello sends her mad, and although the madness is conventionally depicted, it is none the less moving and also used to provide moments which comment acutely on the nature of the society from which she has now withdrawn, as in her inability at first to accept Marcello's death:

Alas he is not dead: he's in a trance.
Why here's nobody shall get anything by his death. Let me call him again for God's sake.

(V.ii.27–8)

Here Cornelia's underlying awareness that in this society deaths are brought about for financial profit supports her feeling that there is no reason in her impoverished son's death, and that he therefore must be alive. At the end of her mournful song, '*Call for the robin red breast and*

the wren,' a haunting vision of human vulnerability and friendlessness,
she returns again to a view of life in commercial terms:

> His wealth is summ'd, and this is all his store:
> This poor men get; and great men get no more.
> Now the wares are gone, we may shut up shop.
>
> (V.iv.108–10)

The last line may imply that Cornelia's son was her 'wares', the only
means she had of supporting herself; now that he is gone, she has nothing
left to barter or sell.

In *The White Devil* the other female characters in their various ways
oppose and criticize Vittoria, redefining her viciousness for the audience
by contrast with themselves. Even Zanche, though seen finally at her
mistress's side in death, is prepared to betray her to the disguised Francisco to further her own interests. It is not only the women who act
towards Vittoria in this way; Flamineo's satire, directed in general
against court society, frequently finds a target in the love of Vittoria and
Brachiano. Her status as a brilliant and desirable woman is constantly
demeaned by her brother's undercutting asides, which relate her behaviour to a syndrome of insulting assumptions based on the commonplace quality of her sexuality:

> Women are caught as you take tortoises,
> She must be turn'd on her back.
>
> Young leverets stand not long; and women's anger
> Should, like their flight, procure a little sport;
> A full cry for a quarter of an hour;
> And then be put to th' dead quat.
>
> (IV.ii.151–2, 159–62)

Even in the play's last scene Flamineo subjects his sister to generalizations of this kind – 'Trust a woman? Never, never; Brachiano be my
precedent: we lay our souls to pawn to the devil for a little pleasure, and
a woman makes the bill of sale. That ever a man should marry!'
(V.vi.158–61). Vittoria's equivocal, but entirely characteristic behaviour
here, in the device of the false suicide pact, allows for the validity of this
view of women as venial and untrustworthy at least on the evidence
provided in the play. If Vittoria is admirable and heroic, it must be in a
way that allows her to share in what the play sees as natural female
weakness common to all womankind, but at the same time to be capable
in addition of what Flamineo calls 'masculine virtue'. Flamineo's view is
not normative; he is a cynical malcontent out for what he can get, but his

conception of Vittoria is supported by other characters, as well as by Webster's presentation of her own behaviour.

The Duchess, on the other hand, is not subject to judgement in quite this way. Of the other two female characters, one knows nothing of her, while the other, Cariola, is admiring rather than critical. Her comments sometimes provide attitudes for the audience to associate themselves with, and in her role of the faithful serving-maid she defines the Duchess as a person worth fidelity. At the end of the first act, after the secret marriage ceremony, Cariola remains onstage alone to deliver a comment on the scene she has witnessed:

> Whether the spirit of greatness or of woman
> Reign most in her, I know not, but it shows
> A fearful madness; I owe her much of pity.

> (I.ii.420–2)

The way in which this comment is presented testifies to its status as a normative or unbiased view; she does not admire the Duchess's action in courting and marrying Antonio uncritically, although she allows that it could be the sign of 'the spirit of greatness' equally well as of what is perhaps its opposite, the spirit of woman. Her response is that which Aristotle thought proper to a tragedy: pity and fear. In the death scene Cariola's loyal efforts to comfort and protect the Duchess and her desire to die with her reflect well on both women; her painful struggles before death illuminate by contrast the Duchess's calm acceptance of suffering and humiliation. Cariola does offer a criticism of her mistress's behaviour at one point, when she objects to the idea, proposed by Bosola, of a feigned pilgrimage to Ancona in order for the Duchess to escape from the Cardinal and Ferdinand. The Duchess is brief with her objection:

> Thou art a superstitious fool:
> Prepare us instantly for our departure.

> (III.ii.319–20)

The response of the audience to this difference of opinion between Cariola and the Duchess must be tempered by irony, because we know that Bosola is the Duchess's enemy at this point and his proposal can only be a plan to trap her. Indeed, she plays directly into her brothers' hands by undertaking the pilgrimage. But at the same time we can hardly feel that had she been more superstitious it would have been better for her; her fatal error has already been made, and she could not have escaped its consequences by staying at home. Other unbiased commentary on her actions comes from the pilgrims at Loretto:

> Here's a strange turn of state: who would have thought
> So great a lady would have match'd herself
> Unto so mean a person? Yet the cardinal
> Bears himself much too cruel.

$$(III.iv.23-6)$$

This simplified summary seems to imply the inadequacy of such judgements by an outsider; this is what the world thinks – is it in any position to know? The second pilgrim uses the loaded word 'looseness' of her:

> They are a free state sir, and her brother show'd
> How that the Pope, forehearing of her looseness,
> Hath seiz'd into th' protection of the Church
> The Dukedom which she held as dowager.

$$(III.iv.29-32)$$

It isn't clear here if the judgement of the Duchess's sexuality is the Cardinal's, the Pope's or the Pilgrim's; perhaps the uncertainty makes the term seem more colourless. In any case, as compared with the tone of the commentary on Vittoria's sexual morality, from a variety of sources in the play, this is very mild.

It is significant that Bosola, Flamineo's equivalent as satiric commentator, though involved with and deeply interested in the Duchess's behaviour, does not comment satirically upon it in the way of Flamineo. He too attacks women, for instance in II.ii declaiming against the use of cosmetics with Hamlet-like venom, but his remarks here are all directly aimed at the Old Lady and her attempts to preserve the appearance of youth by this means. They have no bearing on the Duchess whose physical presence contrastingly evokes only what is natural and unaffected, both in the hair-brushing scene (III.ii) and in the scene of her advanced pregnancy. Bosola's description of her here is graphic but, surprisingly, without any hint of satire or sexual disgust:

> I observe our Duchess
> Is sick a'days, she pukes, her stomach seethes,
> The fins of her eyelids look most teeming blue,
> She wanes i'th' cheek, and waxes fat i'th' flank.

$$(II.i.67-70)$$

He is not characterized by generalizations about female sexuality like Flamineo, whose perverted and voyeuristic tendencies are perhaps reinterpreted in Ferdinand. This is worthy of note in view of Bosola's uninhibited satirical characterizations of Ferdinand and the Cardinal, and the wry pleasure he shows otherwise in what is base and disgusting;

the fantasy about the Old Lady's closet – 'a shop of witchcraft ... in it the fat of serpents; spawn of snakes, Jews' spittle, and their young children's ordure, and all these for the face' – pulls no punches. But he does not direct this sort of language against the Duchess, and once she is dead his is the loudest voice spoken in her praise. It is Ferdinand who is given something of Flamineo's cynicism about women, expressed in generalizations which he relates to his sister:

> Women like that part, which, like the lamprey,
> Hath nev'r a bone in in't.
>
> (I.ii.258–9)

> What cannot a neat knave with a smooth tale
> Make a woman believe?
>
> (I.ii.261–2)

> Foolish men,
> That e'er will trust their honour in a bark,
> Made of so slight, weak bulrush, as is woman,
> Apt every minute to sink it!
>
> (II.v.33–6)

But in his case his involvement with his sister is so intense and passionate that the generalizations have nothing of Flamineo's cold detachment, and express more of Ferdinand himself than of the Duchess. In fact, given the stress placed in Webster's source, William Painter's *The Palace of Pleasure*, novella xxiii, on the Duchess's sexual appetite, her nocturnal longings for pleasure, 'the ticklish instigations of hir wanton flesh', as Painter puts it, Webster would seem to have deliberately reduced the theme of female sexual desire inherent in the story. Antonio extols the Duchess's chastity in hyperbolical terms that draw forth a laughing demurral from Delio:

> in that look
> There speaketh so divine a continence,
> As cuts off all lascivious, and vain hope.
> Her days are practis'd in such noble virtue,
> That, sure her nights, nay more, her very sleeps,
> Are more in heaven, than other ladies' shrifts.
>
> (I.ii.123 8)

Certainly this is not quite how she appears when she woos him later in the scene, but the difference is not one of ironic contrast. It is only Ferdinand who associates her with the stereotype of the 'lusty widow'

(I.ii.262). Otherwise Webster is remarkably reticent in drawing attention to this potentially most vulnerable aspect of her character.

None the less there are similarities between Vittoria and the Duchess, particularly in the treatment of their sexuality. In both cases the catalyst for the main action is not, as in tragedies of blood up to this point, a criminal act, but a sexual liaison which incurs the disapproval not only of society in general but of the woman's family in particular. In *The White Devil* it is more obvious than in *The Duchess of Malfi* that this is disapproval according to masculine standards and from a masculine point of view; Brachiano solicits Vittoria and woos her away from her husband; he is both more powerful and richer than Camillo, and he must necessarily be the active partner in bringing about their love affair. If it is Vittoria who suggests the idea for disposing of their redundant spouses, it is Brachiano who organizes and approves the murders. Yet the trial which forms the central scene of the play is of Vittoria and not Brachiano. Brachiano, although technically more guilty than his mistress on the main charge, ironically attends as a spectator. That his presence is neither expected nor desired by Monticelso and Francisco, who are running the trial, is evident, and Brachiano who, like all Webster's main characters, enjoys theatrical display, luxuriates in the role of 'unbidden guest', making play with the rich gown he spreads out in court on which to sit, leaving it behind with 'the rest o'th' household stuff' in a grand gesture when he departs. He is free to come and go at will, and to make a nonchalant interruption of Vittoria's interrogation with complete impunity. Vittoria, on the other hand, must endure the browbeating and the insults of her accusers; her spirited answers can often be turned against her by Monticelso, who acts, as she points out, both as accuser and judge. It is not only that her way of life can be adduced as circumstantial evidence to substantiate the charges against her, but that, as a woman she cannot be seen to stand up for herself without acting against acceptable standards of womanhood. When Monticelso tries to blacken her character by drawing attention to her fine clothing, she gives an answer which is bold but also logical:

MONTICELSO: look upon this creature was his wife.
                        She comes not like a widow: she comes arm'd
                        With scorn and impudence. Is this a mourning habit?
VITTORIA: Had I foreknown his death as you suggest,
                        I would have bespoke my mourning.

(III.ii.119–23)

The association of fine clothing with immoral behaviour is one that

147

would only be applied to a woman; no mention is made anywhere of
Brachiano's magnificence or ostentatious way of life, for these things are
only to be expected in a Prince. Monticelso responds to Vittoria's defence
with the words, 'O you are cunning,' disregarding its possible validity.
Recognizing that there is no way in which she can acceptably counter
the accusations against her, Vittoria attempts to explain to the court at
large the sexual dilemma in which she finds herself:

> Humbly thus,
> Thus low, to the most worthy and respected
> Lieger ambassadors, my modesty
> And womanhood I tender; but withal
> So entangled in a cursed accusation
> That my defence of force like Perseus,
> Must personate masculine virtue.

> (III.ii.129–35)

'Masculine virtue' is of course unnatural for a woman, and by 'per-
sonating' it, that is, embodying it, Vittoria is moving outside normal
social rules for feminine behaviour. When Francisco recognizes that
they cannot make the charge of murder against Vittoria stick, they have
recourse to a charge relating to Vittoria's contravention of accepted
standards for women, that of incontinence. The incontinence discussed
in the court consists principally of Vittoria's affair with Brachiano in
which, of course, he is equally culpable. Monticelso backs this up with
unproven allegations, stemming, it seems, from Vittoria's lack of dowry:

> 'twas my cousin's fate –
> Ill may I name the hour – to marry you;
> He bought you of your father . . .
> He spent there in six months
> Twelve thousand ducats, and to my acquaintance
> Receiv'd in dowry with you not one julio:
> 'Twas a hard penny-worth, the ware being so light.

> (III.ii.235–41)

Vittoria's 'lightness' in terms of lack of wealth is easily assimilated to
sexual lightness, at least in the eyes of Monticelso and Francisco. No
further evidence seems to be required, other than Vittoria's 'life and
beauty' on which to find her guilty and she is duly sentenced to prison.
Her natural expressions of outrage are quickly dismissed by Monticelso
as raving – 'Fie, she's mad,' 'She's turn'd fury.' A woman can have no
power 'but in the tongue', as Vittoria says (III.ii.283), but if she speaks
too forcibly then she is condemned as shrew or madwoman.

The phrase about 'masculine virtue' reappears in the play on the lips of Flamineo as both of them are dying. In death, Vittoria displays the same qualities as at her trial: courage, boldness, a quick wit and a lively sense of herself as a woman, and a great one. The revengers Lodovico and Gasparo express surprise at her unwomanly bravery, and Vittoria answers punningly:

LODOVICO: Thou dost tremble,
        Methinks fear should dissolve thee into air.
VITTORIA: O thou art deceiv'd, I am too true a woman:
        Conceit can never kill me.

                                 (V.vi.219–22)

'Conceit' here means both apprehension or expectation, vanity, and perhaps also conception, and Vittoria's phrase sounds like a proverb or old joke. By the very act of making herself sound like an ordinary woman in these circumstances she is implicitly drawing attention to what makes her exceptional. Flamineo joins her in mocking their murderers, and brother and sister are at last united in their kinship; now her behaviour can be seen as an extension, rather than as a reversal, of conventional feminine norms:

        Th'art a noble sister,
     I love thee now; if woman do breed man
     She ought to teach him manhood. Fare thee well.

                                 (V.vi.239–41)

There is of course something equivocal in the compliment, as there is when Macbeth praises his wife by desiring her to 'bring forth men children only'. Yet Flamineo recognizes that his sister can be an example to him in a way that is neither peculiarly masculine nor feminine. However, his speech continues with lines that undercut the initial expression of admiration:

        Know many glorious women that are fam'd
     For masculine virtue, have been vicious,
     Only a happier silence did betide them.

                                 (V.vi.242–4)

Does this mean that the 'viciousness' of these women would not matter if it had not been discovered? 'Glorious' sounds like a word that stands outside moral judgement, yet 'glory' implies honour, earned commendation and, when Flamineo uses it again a few lines later in the phrase 'glorious villains', there is clearly a sense of moral paradox. Vittoria is an ambivalent figure to the last, and Webster has presented her in such a way that no easy moral assessments are possible. He highlights her dilemma as a woman whose very success in a man's world brings about her fall; she has no viable assets other than her beauty and sexuality, but she cannot use these to safeguard herself and her family without endangering herself. Her situation has in it aspects of enduring relevance.

The Duchess of Malfi is a woman in a man's world in a different sense. She is not a sexual adventurer like Vittoria, but again it is the expression of her sexuality which puts her in the power of men. Where Vittoria's behaviour is measured against one female sexual stereotype, the courtesan, the Duchess's is measured against another, the widow. Early in the play an ideal of female virtue is embodied in a speech by Antonio, describing the Duchess. He attributes to her two particular qualities: discourse which is 'full of rapture', but not too lengthy, and 'so divine a continence / As cuts off all lascivious, and vain hope'. Just as Desdemona in *Othello* does not live up to her father's ideal of 'a maiden never bold', so the Duchess, in the encounter that is soon to follow with her two brothers, exhibits qualities which counteract Antonio's description. Her speech, though not protracted, is far from pious or submissive, and she answers her brothers' united attack on her with wit and confidence. The triteness of their orchestrated platitudes about second marriage is highlighted by her riposte:

FERDINAND: Marry? they are most luxurious
             Will wed twice.
CARDINAL: O fie!
FERDINAND: Their livers are more spotted
             Than Laban's sheep.
DUCHESS: Diamonds are of most value
             They say, that have pass'd through most jewellers' hands.

                               (I.ii.221–3)

Again, men use generalizations and circumstantial evidence as means of making insinuations against a woman's moral character. The innuendo in Ferdinand's remarks about his sister's court life is crude:

      I would have you give o'er these chargeable revels;
      A visor and a mask are whispering-rooms
      That were nev'r built for goodness: fare ye well:
      And women like that part, which, like the lamprey,
      Hath nev'r a bone in't.

                                 (I.ii.255–9)

Immediately her brothers have left the stage the Duchess is given a defiant little soliloquy asserting her intention to disobey them. Are we tempted here to find some grain of truth in the attitudes of Ferdinand and the Cardinal towards their sister? The juxtaposition might imply this, yet, as has been suggested earlier, the syndrome of the 'lusty widow' is otherwise very little associated with the Duchess, and the brothers' viewpoint is distinctly placed as biased and unnatural. Ferdinand's fantasies about her lover, in the scene where he reacts to the news that she has had a child, do not operate so as to make implications to the audience about her lustful nature: rather the reverse, since Antonio is so different from the 'strong-thigh'd bargeman ... or else some lovely squire' of the Duke's tormented imaginings. The Duchess is not accused or perceived as being guilty of 'incontinence'; nor is she a 'glorious villain' or famed for 'masculine virtue'. In fact the virtuous name which she eventually wins for herself is acquired through a display of several conventionally feminine qualities:

> She's sad, as one long us'd to't: and she seems
> Rather to welcome the end of misery
> Than shun it: a behaviour so noble,
> As gives a majesty to adversity:
> You may discern the shape of loveliness
> More perfect in her tears, than in her smiles;
> She will muse four hours together: and her silence,
> Methinks, expresseth more than if she spake.
>
> (IV.i.2–10)

As Lisa Jardine says, in *Still Harping on Daughters*, 'majesty in the female hero is here at its most reassuring and admirable when associated with patient suffering' (p. 71). The Duchess is resigned, submissive, tearful and silent, yet she manages, in her melancholy, to retain a 'strange disdain' (IV.i.12) that Ferdinand would prefer to eliminate, and it is this which sustains her spirit through the long torment so that she is courageous in the face of death.

Initially she is a woman of some power; as a Duchess and member of a ruling family, head, after her husband's death, of her own household, wealthy in her own right. In this her social position is quite unlike Vittoria's and she has no need to exploit her sexuality to gain security in the same way. Yet she is still vulnerable as a woman in a man's world. She is young, she needs help in running her household, she needs a man at her side. If she is to remarry, she has a duty to her family and her birth. In directly countermanding her brothers' expressed wishes, she is invoking powerful sanctions against herself and her second husband.

151

She acts as if her position as royal widow (to the Duke of Malfi), and Princess in her own right, along with her brothers, of a 'free state', could make her invulnerable and able to determine her own behaviour, but in this she is proved wrong. Because the Cardinal can convince the Pope of her 'looseness' she can be deprived of her Dukedom; when she sends her eldest son and heir away with Antonio (III.v) and is later shown what she believes to be their corpses, she is denuded of all the potential for power and influence she initially believed herself to possess. Even a woman who seems so strong in terms of hereditary rights and worldly possessions as the Duchess at the start of the play can be reduced to impotence and humiliation if she acts in a way that male-dominated society disapproves of. It is as selfless mother that the Duchess makes her greatest appeal for audience sympathy before her death:

> I pray thee look thou giv'st my little boy
> Some syrup for his cold, and let the girl
> Say her prayers, ere she sleep.

(IV.ii.203–5)

This is a role which cannot fail to move the heart. Whereas at the beginning of the play the Duchess with her youth, wealth and undirected sexuality can be seen as posing a threat, not only to the security of her brothers, but more generally to male-dominated society as a woman with certain weapons available to her, in her death she is tamed and reduced; as the poor and suffering Madonna she represents an image of womanhood entirely acceptable. Innocent and dead, she can move Bosola to pity and rouse Ferdinand to guilt and madness; the equivocal associations of the woman she was, wealthy and free, have been entirely purged.

Suggested Reading

1. Editions of *The White Devil* and *The Duchess of Malfi*. All quotations in this study are taken from the Penguin Classics edition of *John Webster. Three Plays*, edited by D. Gunby (Penguin, 1986). *The Complete Works of John Webster*, edited by F. L. Lucas, 4 vols. (London, 1927), though in some ways superseded by more recent scholarship, is still the only complete edition of Webster, and contains extensive introductions, copious annotation and old-spelling texts. Other useful editions are *The White Devil*, ed. J. R. Brown, The Revels Plays (London, 2nd ed., 1966) and *The Duchess of Malfi*, ed. J. R. Brown, The Revels Plays (London, 1964), which are very fully annotated, with excellent introductions, and also *The White Devil*, ed. E. Brennan, New Mermaid Series, Norton Books (London, 1966) and *The Duchess of Malfi*, ed. E. Brennan, New Mermaid Series, Norton Books (London, 1964).

2. R. Berry, *The Art of John Webster*, Oxford, 1972. A stimulating study of Webster's stagecraft, especially in relation to the characteristic forms and attitudes of baroque art.

3. T. Bogard, *The Tragic Satire of John Webster*, Berkeley, California, 1955. Especially useful on Webster's relationship to the drama of his contemporaries.

4. G. Boklund, *The Duchess of Malfi, Sources, Themes, Characters*, Harvard, 1962. A basic study of Webster's treatment of his source-material.

5. G. Boklund, *The Sources of The White Devil*. Essays and Studies on English Language and Literature, Uppsala, 1957. An exhaustive scholarly study of the complex problems of the source-material of this play.

6. M. Bradbrook, *John Webster Citizen and Dramatist*, London, 1980. A critical biography of Webster, incorporating the results of recent research into the facts of Webster's life, and setting the plays in their Jacobean context.

7. A. Dallby, *The Anatomy of Evil. A Study of John Webster's 'The White Devil'*, Land, Malmo, 1974. The fullest study of this play to date, with much useful material on the play's structure and dramatic techniques.

8. R. W. Dent, *John Webster's Borrowing*, University of California Press, 1960. Though Dent's findings have now been supplemented by those of others (e.g. J. R. Brown, no. 1 above, and G. Boklund, nos. 4 and 5 above) this remains a seminal book on Webster's verbal debts.

9. I. S. Ekeblad, 'The Impure Art of John Webster', *Review of English Studies* n.s. ix (1958), pp. 253–67. A valuable article on the movement between convention and realism in *The Duchess of Malfi*, with a detailed analysis of IV.ii, showing how its structure imitates by parody that of a marriage-masque.

10. U. Ellis-Fermor, *The Jacobean Drama*, London, 1936, 1965. Contains a profoundly perceptive chapter on the qualities of Webster's art and the nature of his spiritual universe.

11. L. Jardine, *Still Harping on Daughters*, Brighton, 1982. Contains an excellent article on *The Duchess of Malfi* from a feminist standpoint, especially concerned with her role as an inheritor of wealth.

12. J. W. Lever, *The Tragedy of State*, London, 1971. A challenging view of the depiction of society and power relations within Jacobean drama, in which Webster's tragedies are interpreted as critiques of the corruption in public life.

13. J. R. Mulryne, '*The White Devil* and *The Duchess of Malfi*', in *Jacobean Theatre*, Stratford-upon-Avon Studies 1, 1960, pp. 200–25. A compressed and suggestive comparative treatment of the two plays.

14. R. Ornstein, *The Moral Vision of Jacobean Tragedy*, Madison and Milwaukee, 1960. Contains a perceptive treatment of Webster's moral art in which these two plays are seen as 'the last Jacobean tragedies of heroic proportion'.

15. H. T. Prince, 'The Function of Imagery in Webster'. *PMLA*, LXX (1955), pp. 717–39. A seminal and much-cited article developing his view of the unique and, as he calls it, 'resolute' consistency with which Webster elaborates his imagery into a coherent sequence.

FOR THE BEST IN PAPERBACKS, LOOK FOR THE 🐧

In every corner of the world, on every subject under the sun, Penguins represent quality and variety – the very best in publishing today.

For complete information about books available from Penguin and how to order them, write to us at the appropriate address below. Please note that for copyright reasons the selection of books varies from country to country.

In the United Kingdom: For a complete list of books available from Penguin in the U.K., please write to *Dept EP, Penguin Books Ltd, Harmondsworth, Middlesex, UB7 0DA*

In the United States: For a complete list of books available from Penguin in the U.S., please write to *Dept BA, Viking Penguin, 299 Murray Hill Parkway, East Rutherford, New Jersey 07073*

In Canada: For a complete list of books available from Penguin in Canada, please write to *Penguin Books Canada Limited, 2801 John Street, Markham, Ontario L3R 1B4*

In Australia: For a complete list of books available from Penguin in Australia, please write to the *Marketing Department, Penguin Books Australia Ltd, P.O. Box 257, Ringwood, Victoria 3134*

In New Zealand: For a complete list of books available from Penguin in New Zealand, please write to the *Marketing Department, Penguin Books (N.Z.) Ltd, Private Bag, Takapuna, Auckland 9*

In India: For a complete list of books available from Penguin in India, please write to *Penguin Overseas Ltd, 706 Eros Apartments, 56 Nehru Place, New Delhi 110019*

FOR THE BEST IN PAPERBACKS, LOOK FOR THE 🐧

PENGUIN PASSNOTES

This comprehensive series, designed to help O-level and CSE students, includes:

SUBJECTS
Biology
Chemistry
Economics
English Language
French
Geography
Human Biology
Mathematics
Modern Mathematics
Modern World History
Narrative Poems
Physics

SHAKESPEARE
As You Like It
Henry IV, Part I
Henry V
Julius Caesar
Macbeth
The Merchant of Venice
A Midsummer Night's Dream
Romeo and Juliet
Twelfth Night

LITERATURE
Arms and the Man
Cider With Rosie
Great Expectations
Jane Eyre
Kes
Lord of the Flies
A Man for All Seasons
The Mayor of Casterbridge
My Family and Other Animals
Pride and Prejudice
The Prologue to The Canterbury
    Tales
Pygmalion
Saint Joan
She Stoops to Conquer
Silas Marner
To Kill a Mockingbird
War of the Worlds
The Woman in White
Wuthering Heights